Religion and Science:
God, Evolution and the Soul
by
Nancey Murphy

Religion and Science:
God, Evolution and the Soul
by
Nancey Murphy

Proceedings of
the Goshen Conference
on Religion and Science

Carl S. Helrich, Editor

National Library of Canada Cataloguing in Publication

Goshen Conference on Religion and Science (2001 : Goshen, Ind.)
    Religion and science : God, evolution and the soul by Nancey
Murphy: proceedings of the Goshen Conference on Religion and Science /
Carl S. Helrich, editor.

ISBN 1-894710-20-7

    1. Religion and science—Congresses. 2. Natural theology—
Congresses. 3. Evolution—Religious aspects—Mennonites—Congresses.
I. Murphy, Nancey C. II. Helrich, Carl S. III. Title.

BL241.G68 2001   261.5'5   C2002-902723-3

RELIGION AND SCIENCE: GOD, EVOLUTION AND THE SOUL BY NANCEY
MURPHY: PROCEEDINGS OF THE GOSHEN CONFERENCE ON RELIGION AND
SCIENCE

Copyright©2002 by Pandora Press
        Kitchener, Ont. N2G 3R2
        All rights reserved
Co-published with Herald Press,
        Scottdale, Pennsylvania; Waterloo, Ontario
International Standard Book Number: 1-894710-20-7
Printed in Canada on acid-free paper
Cover design by Clifford Snyder
Book design by Julia Stark

11 10 09 08 07 06 05 04 03 02   10 9 8 7 6 5 4 3 2 1

Table of Contents

Conference Participation
By Institution

The institutions of higher education represented at the conference included:

John Carroll University (OH), Purdue University (IN), Zygon Center for Religion and Science (IL), Goshen College (IN), Portland State University (OR), University of Illinois (IL), Taylor University, Bluffton College (OH), Garrett-Evangelical Theological Seminary (IL), Anderson University (IN), Grand Valley State University (MI), Eastern Mennonite University (VA), Fuller Theological Seminary (CA), St. Thomas Aquinas Center (IN), Loyola College of Maryland (MD), and Bethel College (KS).

Acknowledgements

"God's Nonviolent Direct Action" was published previously in *Reading the Universe Through Science, Religion, and Ethics*, ed. C. W. du Toit (Pretoria: Research Institute for Theology and Religion, 1999). It is republished here with the kind permission of the Research Institute for Theology and Religion.

Editor's Preface

This first Goshen College[1] Conference on Religion and Science was modeled after the very successful series of Cosmos and Creation conferences held annually at Loyola College of Maryland. The format followed by those conferences has provided the context for a free and open discussion. Since interaction and discussion were desired as characteristics of the Goshen conference, the Cosmos and Creation format was adhered to rather closely.

The genius of the Cosmos and Creation format is the use of a single speaker and the opportunity for interaction with that speaker. The speaker for this first Goshen conference was Professor Nancey Murphy of the Fuller Theological Seminary. Her presentations included two public lectures and one internal lecture for which the audience consisted only of the conference participants.

The Conference began on Friday evening with a reception and meal in the Fellowship Hall of the Goshen College Mennonite Church. This was followed by the first public lecture presented by Professor Murphy in the Chapel. An open question and answer period, which was not recorded, followed the lecture. Saturday morning began with a discussion among the conference participants and Professor Murphy. The topic was primarily the evening lecture. A second public lecture followed. Discussion of this took place in the afternoon in the same closed setting with participants and Professor Murphy. The third (internal) lecture and discussion concluded the conference.

One difference between the Goshen and the Loyola conferences is the fact that the Loyola conference has a Catholic spirit, or flavor, while that of the Goshen conference is Mennonite. This is not evidenced directly in the discussions, or in the lectures. The Goshen faculty involved in this conference attempted, however, to provide this flavor at other junctures. Professor Don Blosser of the Goshen College department of Bible Religion and Philosophy graciously consented to provide leadership for the Saturday afternoon (Vespers) service, following the discussion, and the Sunday morning worship. At Don's suggestion the Vespers service was held in the same room where the discussion had taken place, since for Mennonites the place of worship is hallowed by communion with God. The place of worship need not be separated from the place of work. The Sunday worship was held in what was once the Chapel of the Goshen Seminary. Mennonite worship is simple in form, making little or no distinction between pastor and congregation. The Sunday worship involved students as well as faculty. Don presented the traditional brief message.

Students were invited to participate in the conference. In the Cosmos tradition, the discussions were at a fairly high level. Therefore there was a mild selection procedure in the invitation of students. Because of the educational requirements in religion at Goshen College, and because of the atmosphere of the campus, the Goshen student is normally prepared to engage in many of the issues considered in the conference. But the difference in chronological age and educational preparation between student and faculty could not be ignored. We shall continue to have student participation in this conference and shall attempt to be creative in providing for that.

The written copies of the papers printed here were provided directly by Professor Murphy. These include the two public lectures presented on Friday evening and Saturday morning of the conference as well as the internal lecture given Sunday morning. The internal lecture, "Evolution: One Anabaptist's Perspective," was not previously written in polished form. As late as Saturday evening Professor Murphy said that she knew generally what she wanted to say, but was not then certain of the details. So the conference participants had the privilege of a lively and fresh presentation on Sunday morning. The form of the lecture printed here was first transcribed from the tapes of the conference and then edited and corrected by Professor Murphy. This is the first publication of that lecture.

All of the discussions were taped, with the exception of those on Friday evening, which were not recorded because of a communication failure. In this first conference the positioning of microphones and the subsequent recording of all comments and contributions was not ideal. So the editing of the discussions was a challenging undertaking. In some instances it was simply not possible to understand what was said, and some liberty was exercised in the final written transcript. I accept full responsibility for any errors in representation of any of the ideas.

I have tried also to provide some of the freshness of the discussion in the printed record. That, of course, cannot be completely conveyed to anyone who was not an actual participant. The Old Testament scholarship of one of the Mennonite participants, and the insightful comments of a Jesuit from John Carroll will be easily remembered by conference participants. There were also problems in being able to hear one another because of the room in which the discussions took place. This resulted in comments among the participants, which actually led, in many instances, to a better understanding and appreciation for one another as people. Of necessity much of this is absent from the transcript. But bringing the experience back to our minds is an important goal of any record of proceedings. Therefore, even recognizing the limitations in any such attempt, I have included some instances of laughter and offhand comments in the transcript. It is my hope that this will increase the understanding of readers who were participants and will not be a hindrance to others.

In the transcript of the discussions square brackets, [...], are used to indicate additions made to the actual recorded discussion. This addition has been kept to a minimum and is only to provide a fluid text. The laughter of conference participants is included in parentheses, (...). Professor Murphy occasionally responded to participant comments with the standard "umhmm" of conversation. This has been included directly in the transcript, followed by and added [yes].

With the exception of Professor Murphy, all speakers in the discussions are designated by numbers, such as "Speaker 3." These numbers are uniform throughout the discussions. That is, Speaker 3 in the Saturday morning session is the same person as Speaker 3 in the

Sunday morning session. A key to the speakers has been provided to all conference participants, but is not available publicly.

The index includes reference to the ideas of the various speakers during the discussions. This has been done to facilitate the finding of certain discussions. The participants will remember these, and inclusion of them in the index will help participants to find that little comment they remember. For others it will serve to find those aspects of the discussion they find particularly interesting and will help to identify Nancey Murphy's thoughts on particular topics.

This conference would not have been possible without the vision and generosity of Betty (Miller) and Marlin Jeschke in the Establishment of the Miller-Jeschke Program for Christian Faith and the Natural Sciences. The Miller-Jeschke program has underwritten this conference and provided complete support for Nancey Murphy. This is acknowledged with gratitude.

It is my sincere hope that this Proceedings of the first Goshen Conference on Religion and Science will be of benefit in our individual scholarly work and will convey, in some sense, the atmosphere and hospitality of Goshen College.

Carl S. Helrich
Goshen College
Goshen, Indiana
December, 2001

Lectures

This section contains the lectures presented by Nancey Murphy. The first two were open to the public. The third was presented only to conference participants. Nancey Murphy has edited all of these lectures into the form presented here. Each of these lectures was followed by a discussion session devoted primarily to consideration of that lecture. Of course, as the conference developed the discussion included any and all lectures. The lectures appear in order of delivery and are:

Science, Anabaptism and Theological Anthropology

God's Nonviolent Direct Action

Evolution: One Anabaptist's Perspective

I.
Science, Anabaptism, and Theological Anthropology

Nancey Murphy
April 6, 2001

1. Introduction

My primary academic interest for the past few years has been theories of human nature. In connection with my lectures on this subject to various audiences I've been amazed to discover how much disagreement there is on this subject. To see if that holds true here, as well, I'm going to ask you to respond to a little survey. This is multiple choice; I'll tell you the four options, then ask for a show of hands.

> *Which of the following comes closest to your view of human nature?*
> *1. Humans are composed of three parts; e.g., body, soul, and spirit: (trichotomism).*
>
> *2. Humans are composed of two parts: (dualism).*
>   *2a. A body and a soul.*
>   *2b. A body and a mind.*
> *3. Humans are composed of one "part": a physical body (physicalism).*
> *4. None of the above*

Usually I find trichotomists in the majority, followed by dualists, and only a few physicalists and others.

This is an important issue, then, to get out on the table. It is clear that this often-unnamed conflict has consequences for morality and public policy. I suspect that it lies at the heart of the current debate over the use of fetal stem cells for research. Because of the religious basis for most trichotomism and dualism there is a danger that this issue will reinforce the all-too-common perception that science and religion are intrinsic enemies. That is, while some philosophers have argued for physicalism for centuries, developments in neuroscience have brought these arguments into the public arena and these scientific developments provide strong support for physicalism.

My plan this evening is to provide a historical sketch of theories of human nature in the West, followed by a glimpse of the scientific developments that support a physicalist account of human nature. I'll then comment on some of the theological issues at stake and end with reflections on why this issue should be of particular interest to those of us in the Anabaptist tradition.

2. History

I have failed to discover any comprehensive history of the issue with which I'm concerned here – the metaphysical make up of the human person. One aspect that needs to be included is the history of *oversimplifications* of earlier history – to which I hope I am not now contributing! Nonetheless, here is my amateur historian's account.

Apparently there were a variety of theories of human nature, with correlative expectations regarding death, available to the writers of the New Testament. It is widely agreed among current Christian and Jewish scholars that early Hebraic accounts of the person were holistic and physicalist, and there was no well-developed account of life after death. By Jesus' day, however, there was a lively debate as to whether or not the dead would rise at the end of time. The Hellenization of the region had begun several centuries earlier and some Jews had adopted a dualistic view of body and soul, along with a conception of the soul's survival of death. Early Gentile Christians probably held an even wider variety of views. The important fact to note is that there is no explicit teaching on the metaphysical composition of the person;[2] however, the New Testament writers did clearly emphasize the resurrection of the body (as opposed to immortality of the soul) as a guarantee of life after death. Writing to the church at Corinth, Paul's apology for the resurrection of the body met resistance from some who found it too good to be true and from others who could not understand why they should *want* to be encumbered again by a body once they had escaped it at death.

In fact, J. D. G. Dunn argues that the very questions we address to the texts about the various constitutive parts of the person are foreign to biblical thought. He distinguishes between partitive and aspective understanding, the latter being the tendency of the Bible. Here one speaks of the whole person from various aspects, or in light of the person's various relationships to something else. So what appears to us as a part, for example, the body, is a term for the whole person thought of from a certain angle.³ Biblical anthropology is concerned about relationships – to others, to the natural world, and to God.

However, As Christianity spread throughout the Mediterranean world and its theology was developed in conversation with a variety of philosophical and religious systems, a modified Neoplatonic account of the person came to predominate in scholarly circles. The *eternal* Platonic soul became (merely) immortal and there was added the expectation that it would be reunited with a body at the end of time. Augustine's account was the most influential until the later Middle Ages.

A major turning point in Christian history was a result of borrowing from Muslim scholarship in the later Middle Ages. I shall return shortly to Thomas Aquinas's account of the soul, with its dependence on Aristotle and on further developments by Muslim scholars. Thomas's position, based on Aristotle's conception of the soul as the form of the body, may be described as a modified rather than radical dualism.

Two factors at the dawn of modernity challenged the Aristotelian account of human nature. One was the mainline Protestant Reformation's tendency to associate Aristotle with Catholicism and to return to the more Platonic elements in Augustine's thought. The other was the demise of Aristotelian metaphysics as a whole as a result of the rise of modern science – the substitution of atomism for hylomorphism. In response, René Descartes provided modern Europeans with a dualism of mind and body even more radical than Plato's – mental substance is defined *over against* material substance, and the body is purely mechanical.

The interesting twists in this story are the result of critical church history and historical-critical biblical scholarship, beginning especially in the nineteenth century. At that time many scholars called into question the authenticity of miracle accounts in the Bible, and especially the chief miracle, the resurrection of Jesus. This led to an emphasis in theological circles on an immortal soul as the only basis for Christian hope for life after death. Immanuel Kant's transcendental argument for the immortality of the soul played a complementary role.

At the same time, though, critical scholarship made it possible to ask whether current doctrine (including doctrines regarding the soul) were in fact original Christian (and Hebraic) teaching, or whether they were the result of later doctrinal development read back into the biblical texts. It became common during the twentieth century to make a sharp distinction between original Hebraic conceptions and later Greek accretions such as body-soul dualism, and to favor the former as authentic Christian teaching. In addition, both theologians and biblical scholars in the past generation have rediscovered the centrality of the resurrection of the body in primitive Christian proclamation. While the sharp distinction between Greek and Hebraic thought was later called into question, the recognition of the importance of bodily resurrection stands as a permanent achievement.[4]

3. Science and the Soul

Science has affected these debates at three major points. First, as already mentioned, the atomist revolution in physics represented the replacement of Aristotelian hylomorphism, so not only did it become impossible to understand soul as the form of the body, but the very conception of matter involved in speaking of the body changed radically. Second, evolutionary biology pushed many in the direction of physicalist accounts of human nature: if animals have no souls (as moderns, beginning with Descartes, assumed) then humans must not have them either. But others argued that the concept of soul is all the more important in order to account for human distinctiveness. The thesis of this paper is that the most significant scientific development having a bearing on this long history of debates is now occurring in the cognitive-neurosciences. But first, a quick look at evolutionary biology.

3.1 Darwin and Dualism

Already in Darwin's day the theory of evolution raised the possibility that humanity and all its works, including society and culture, could be explained in purely biological terms. If so, free will and responsibility seemed to be in jeopardy. To protect the dignity of humans, many relied on the mind-body (or body-soul) dualism that had been employed since the rise of modern physics to attempt to exempt human freedom and intelligence from the blind determination of natural laws. It became a common strategy among Christians to reconcile theological and biological accounts of human nature by granting that the human *body* may well have evolved from animals, but to insist that human distinctiveness is a function of the *soul*, specially created by God.

It may have been reasonable in Darwin's day to imagine that there was some point in evolutionary history when the first human body was conceived and that God began at that point to create human souls. That is, humans were said to have evolved from apes, and it made sense to assume that humans had souls but apes did not. (However, this image cannot be pressed too far: was the first human infant borne by a soulless ape?) Current accounts of the evolution of humans make this notion of "soul insertion" even less plausible.

We can now trace human origins to an extinct common ancestor of both humans and apes, a creature that lived five to seven million years ago. Between then and now there have been a variety of hominid species. The first known hominid, *Ardipithecus ramidus*, lived 4.4 Mya but it is not clear whether it is in the direct line of descent to modern humans. Those known to be our ancestors include *Australopithecus anamensis*, *Australopithecus afarensis*, *Homo habilis*, and *Homo erectus*. There are other hominids not in the direct line of descent to modern humans such as *Australopithecus africanus*. Between three and one Mya, three or four hominid species lived contemporaneously in the African continent. More recently, Neanderthal hominids, with brains as large as ours, lived contemporaneously with modern humans.[5] The burial practices and cave drawings of Neanderthals are often taken to show religious awareness.

So did all hominids have souls, or only those in the direct line of descent of *Homo sapiens?* What about the Neanderthals? Or was it only modern humans? The very oddity of these questions may lead to a suspicion that evolution and dualism are odd bedfellows.

3.2 Neuroscience and the Soul

It is said that Darwin completed the Copernican revolution, bringing living things within the purview of the natural sciences. If this is the case, then one might add that contemporary neuroscience is now completing the Darwinian revolution, bringing the mind within the purview of biology. The development of new brain imaging techniques, along with new techniques for computer modeling of cognitive processes, made the 1990s the "decade of the brain." My claim, in short, is this: all of the human capacities once attributed to the immaterial mind or soul are now yielding to the insights of neurobiology. To see this, though, we need a clear account of just what it is that the soul has been thought to do.

One of the most elaborate and perceptive accounts of the functions of the soul was that of Thomas Aquinas.[6] He followed Aristotle in recognizing three levels of functioning: that which we share with both animals and plants, that which we share with only the animals, and that which is distinctive of humans. The faculties attributed to the lowest aspect of the soul – nutrition, growth, and reproduction – have long fallen within the sphere of biological explanation.

A number of the faculties we share with animals have also been understood biologically for some time: locomotion and sense perception. Neuroscientists have located the motor cortex, auditory and visual cortices, olfactory lobes, and so forth. Another capacity we share with the higher animals is emotion. It was once thought that all emotions were mediated by the same neural machinery, the "limbic system," but more recent research suggests that there are different systems for different emotions.[7]

In addition to the five exterior senses, Thomas postulated four "interior senses" and these capacities show up in particularly interesting ways in contemporary neuroscientific research. The *sensus communis* (common sense) is the faculty that distinguishes and collates the data from the exterior senses – for example, associating the sweetness of honey, its color, texture, and scent in order to allow for recognition of the substance. In contemporary neuroscience an explanation for this ability is referred to as "the binding problem," and it is considered one of the most difficult problems in current research, second only, perhaps, to the problem of consciousness itself.

One of the relevant questions here has to do with how the brain comes to recognize patterns. Do brains come equipped with individual neurons designed for recognizing patterns – that is, a "grandmother neuron" devoted to recognition of one particular elderly woman, and other cells for each pattern that the brain is able to distinguish? It is now believed that recognition tasks depend on activation of large nets or assemblies of neurons rather than on the firing of individual neurons. The concept of a "cell assembly" was introduced by Donald Hebb, and its formation is described as follows: "Any frequently repeated, particular stimulation will lead to the slow development of a 'cell-assembly,' a diffuse structure comprising cells ... capable of acting briefly as a closed system...."[8]

For an example of a capacity that is more readily yielding to research, consider a second of Thomas's interior senses, the *vis aestimativa* (translated as the estimative power or instinctive judgment). This faculty allows for apprehensions that go beyond sensory perception, apprehending, for example, the fact that something is useful, or friendly or unfriendly. One relevant area of research is the investigation of the neural basis for recognition of intentions in both humans and animals. Humans and other social animals come equipped with neural systems that predispose them to pick out faces. The amygdala has been shown to be necessary for interpreting facial expressions, direction of gaze, and tone of voice. Neurons in the same region are responsive to the sight of hands and leg motions typical of walking. Thus, there are neurons whose function is to respond to visual stimuli that indicate the intentions of other agents.[9]

Among the rational faculties distinctive of humans, Thomas distinguished the active and passive intellects. The passive intellect is a sort of memory, closely resembling what current neuroscientists call declarative memory, and this has been found to be dependent on the medial temporal lobe of the brain. Active intellect is responsible for abstracting concepts from sensory experience and for reasoning and judging. These latter capacities are less well understood in neurobiological terms. However, they all involve the use of language, and language use and acquisition are an important area of current study. Two regions of the brain, Wernicke's area and Broca's area, have long been known to be involved in language. Language memory involves a variety of regions; selective damage due to strokes or tumors shows that access to common nouns, proper names, verbs, and even color terms depends on separate regions.[10] Furthermore, syntactic and semantic capacities depend on different regions of the brain.[11]

The third of Thomas's rational faculties is the will. This he defined as the capacity to be attracted to goods of a non-sensory sort. Along with intellect, this is the seat of moral capacities. Furthermore, since God is the ultimate good, the will also accounts for the capacity to be attracted to God. Neuroscience now contributes to our understanding of both morality and religious experience. Antonio Damasio has studied the neural processes that go into practical reasoning, that is, the ability to make both moral and prudential judgments. In his book, *Descartes' Error*, he reports the case of a nineteenth-century railway worker, Phineas Gage, whose brain was pierced by a metal rod.

Gage recovered physically and his cognitive functions (attention, perception, memory, reasoning, language) were all intact. Yet he suffered a dramatic character change after the accident. The doctor who treated him noted that he had become "fitful, irreverent, indulging at times in the grossest profanity which was not previously his custom, manifesting but little deference for his fellows, impatient of restraint or advice when it conflicts with his desires, at times pertinaciously obstinate, yet capricious and vacillating, devising many plans of future operation, which are no sooner arranged than they are abandoned."[12] Damasio's wife Hanna was able to determine from the damage to Gage's skull exactly which parts of the brain would have been destroyed in the accident – selected areas of his prefrontal cortices. Damasio concludes from this and other similar cases that this area of the brain is "concerned specifically with unique human properties, among them: the ability to anticipate the future and plan accordingly within a complex social environment; the sense of responsibility toward the self and others; and the ability to orchestrate one's survival deliberately, at the command of one's free will."[13] In short, what Thomas described as the "appetite for the good" appears to depend directly on localizable brain functions.

A number of neuroscientists have begun to study the role of the brain in religious experience. For example, patients with temporal lobe epilepsy often develop strong interests in religion, and this has led to speculation that the temporal lobes are involved in certain sorts of normal religious experiences as well.[14]

What are we to make of all this? It is important to note that no such accumulation of data can ever amount to a proof that there is no nonmaterial mind or soul in addition to the body. However, if we recognize that the concept of the soul was originally introduced into Western thought as an *explanation* for capacities that appeared not to be explainable in biological terms, then we can certainly say that for scientific purposes the hypothesis has been shown to be unnecessary.

A second caution is in order. It would be easy at this point to fall into the reductionist's error of claiming that "morality" or "religious experience" is *nothing but* a brain process. However, the fact that acting according to an ethical principle requires the participation of brain circuitry does not invalidate the principle. The problem of reductionism in general is one of the most challenging and interesting. I can't give an adequate response here, but let me make one suggestion to help distinguish between a reductive and a non-reductive view of the person. There are two routes by which to arrive at a physicalist account of human beings. One is to begin with dualism, say, of a Cartesian sort, and then subtract the mind or soul, along with the soul's traditional functions. The other route begins with science. We recognize a certain "layered" feature of reality: subatomic particles at the lowest level combine in increasingly complex structures to give us the features of the world known to chemists, and these in turn combine into incredibly complex organizations to give us biological organisms.

The version of physicalism I espouse argues that, just as life appears as a result of complex organization, so too sentience and consciousness appear as nonreducible products of biological organization. To conceive of how it is possible to get "mind" out of matter one needs to appreciate not only the development from inorganic to organic, but also from mere homeostasis, through goal-directedness, information processing, goal evaluation, consciousness, and sociality to self-consciousness.

There are a variety of benefits in approaching physicalism scientifically rather than through a reaction against Cartesianism. An important one is that arguments against the reducibility of the mental to the physical can draw upon parallel arguments against reductionism in other scientific domains.

4. Theological Implications

I want to reflect now on the theological implications of these developments. Given that most theologians throughout much of Christian history have been dualists of one sort or another, there are a number of theological issues that will have to be revisited if a physicalist account of the person is substituted for body-soul dualism.

First, the so-called intermediate state. A controversial issue that needs to be addressed in Catholic and Reformed contexts is the claim that between death and the general resurrection souls have conscious awareness of God. This issue became prominent during the Reformation in connection with controversies over purgatory and the expectation of the imminent return of Christ. The problem is that if there is no substantial soul to survive bodily death then what is to be made of this doctrine? Many reformers, especially within the radical wing, argued that the soul "sleeps" prior to the resurrection and the Last Judgment.

Since "sleep" is a euphemism in the New Testament for death, there are actually two possibilities here – that the soul actually dies with the body or that it is, in some sense, asleep. Some, such as the Polish Anabaptist Simon Budny, taught the more radical view that the soul is but the life of the body and thus ceases to exist at death. More commonly, the radicals taught that the soul continues to exist, yet in an unconscious state.[15]

John Calvin attacked both sorts of views, beginning with a treatise called *Psychopannychia* (1545). This word means a watchful or sentient "wake" of the soul, but nonetheless has come to be associated instead with the two positions Calvin was opposing.[16] Calvin's teaching on the conscious intermediate state has settled this issue for many of his followers. The same teaching had been made official for Catholicism by the Fifth Lateran council in 1513.

So it appears that a nonreductive physicalist account of the person presents problems for Christians of both the Catholic and Reformed traditions. If there is no soul, and the nervous system is the seat of consciousness, then how can there be a wakeful state between death and resurrection? One approach open to those who want to maintain this doctrine is to question the meaningfulness of a time-line in discussing eschatological issues. That is, we presume that God is, in some sense, "outside" of time. If those who have died are "with God" we cannot meaningfully relate their experience to our creaturely history. (When my students ask me about this "doctrine" I tell them that Brethren don't have doctrines, and if we did, this wouldn't be one of them!)

A central and uncontentious theological issue is the importance of the doctrine of the resurrection of the body. I have already pointed out that, while resurrection of the body had been for centuries a mere adjunct to a doctrine of the immortality of the soul, it has now been recognized as central to the gospel proclamation.

Recognition of the centrality of resurrection to Christian teaching, combined with recognition of the continuity of humans with the whole of nature, calls for reconsideration of the scope of God's final transformative act. There is increased motive to agree with theologians, such as Wolfhart Pannenberg, who argue that the resurrection of Jesus is a foretaste of the transformation awaiting the entire cosmos.[17] Paul hints at this in Romans: "For the creation waits with eager longing for the revealing of the children of God; for the creation was subjected to futility, not of its own will but by the will of the one who subjected it, in hope that the creation itself will be set free from its bondage to decay and will obtain the freedom of the glory of the children of God" (Rom. 8:19-21).

The metaphysical make-up of the person is but one aspect of a much broader topic of theological concern, now designated "Christian anthropology." An important theological task is to trace the consequences of a physicalist account of the person for the variety of issues that fall under this heading: one, as mentioned above, is the place of humankind in the rest of nature; others are the source and nature of human sinfulness, and the claim that humans are made in the image of God. Let me address the first of these at some length.

James McClendon agrees that the value of the scientific findings addressed above is to point Western Christians back to a more biblical view of the human race – one that recognizes that, as with the other animals, God formed humans from the dust of the ground. In English we lose the Hebrew pun in calling the first human *adam* because he is formed from *adamah*, dust or ground (Gen. 2:7). We can recapture the imagery if we think of ourselves as *humans*, made from *humus*. In the Genesis stories of creation the only clear difference between the human animal and the others is this: "this creature is *addressed* by the creator." McClendon writes, "[o]ur life as Christians *is* our life as organic constituents of the crust of this planet."[18]

One might ask why this recognition of our physicality is important from a theological perspective. One reason has been spelled out at length in McClendon's *Ethics:* no account of Christian morality that neglects our embodied selfhood can do justice to gospel ethics. A second reason is spelled out in *Doctrine:* it is impossible to do justice to God's relation to the natural world without an appreciation of humans' role in nature. The whole of modern theology has suffered from an anthropocentrizing tendency. Whereas earlier generations had perceived a "living" universe in which spirit and matter were closely intertwined, Descartes and his fellow scientists of the seventeenth century adopted a mechanical model of the universe. This not only created problems for theologians in understanding human nature, but also affected their accounts of the role of God in nature. Many modern theologians relegated nature to the realm of the secular. According to Rudolf Bultmann, nature is an object, entirely governed by natural laws; the religious value of creation is strictly limited since the authentic dependence and freedom that humans can feel and must face not nature, but God only. Ironically, while the architects of this anthropocentric doctrine of creation believed they were protecting faith from alien elements, the unhappy outcome was the banishing of God from nature.[19]

Yet this separation of humankind from its organic family can legitimately be maintained, after Darwin, only by associating our essential humanness with something other than the body and, as shown above, it is becoming increasingly difficult to conceive of what this other element might be. This result is to be celebrated, says McClendon: when humans are seen as part and parcel of nature, then, and only then, can communion with God be seen as the *telos* of the whole evolutionary (and cosmic) process, and nature's trials, too, can be taken up into divine reconciliation. I'll speak to this in my lecture tomorrow. "Creation, the whole of it, has a goal, and that goal lies in God."[20]

One further theological issue: Nicholas Lash argues that a doctrine of God is always correlative to anthropology. When the human person is identified with a solitary mind, God tends to be conceived as a *disembodied* mind, as in the case of classical theism. Much of Lash's own writing argues for the recovery of an embodied and social anthropology in order to recapture a more authentic account of religious experience, but also of a thoroughly Trinitarian concept of God.[21]

There are equally important issues to be re-examined in related areas of Christian thought. The concept of the soul has played a major role in the history of Christian ethics for centuries, for example, as justification for prohibition of abortion and for differential treatment of animals and humans. Where do these arguments stand with a revised concept of the nature of the person? While some fear that the loss of the concept of soul will have a negative impact on Christian ethics, I see it as a valuable stimulus to turn back to the teachings of Jesus for moral guidance. His command to care for "the least of the brethren" would seem to provide adequate grounds for a protection of all human life.

The soul has also long been the focus of spiritual direction and pastoral counseling. What becomes of traditional concepts of religious experience if the person is understood to be purely physical? There have been reactions in recent years against the asceticism fostered by Platonic dualism as well as against the tendency to distinguish between saving souls and caring for people's physical needs. Feminist writers have been critical of accounts of gender relationships in which a superior rational soul has been associated with the masculine, and a subordinate material body with the feminine. In my classes I encourage my students to become aware of the extent to which their experience of God is actually made up largely of bodily experiences: joy, tears, an urge to bow before the Lord.

Another question: How is God's revelation to humans to be understood if humans are body rather than "spirit?" In short, we have to accept the fact that God has to do with brains – crude though this may sound.

Clearly, there is much room for development of more holistic approaches to all of these issues.

However, I've promised to reflect on the particular difference these issues make for Anabaptists. I take it we can assume that the radical reformers did a better job than either the mainline Protestant or Catholic reformers in returning to primitive (and we would say, normative) Christianity. We would also say that original Christianity is better understood in socio-political terms than in terms of what is currently thought of as religious or metaphysical. (I'm greatly indebted to John Howard Yoder's reading of the New Testament here). This is my thesis in brief: The adoption of dualist anthropology provided something different – different from socio-political and ethical concerns – for Christianity to be basically all *about*. The focus on the soul allowed for a shift from this-worldly to transcendent, metaphysical preoccupations.

My reflections here grow out of two sources. One is my own longstanding puzzlement about how the different sorts of Christianity I have encountered can be so different, despite so much doctrinal agreement. For example, the forms of life of my church, the Church of the Brethren, are rather well summed up in the denomination's motto: Continuing the work of Jesus, peacefully, simply, together. Yet at Fuller Seminary, while most of my students are in fact continuing the work of Jesus, their understanding is that Christianity is basically about something else – having one's sins forgiven and eternal life.

The second source of my reflections is David Kelsey's book, *The Uses of Scripture in Recent Theology*. He attributes differences among theologies and approaches to scriptural authority to different ideas about how to construe God's presence in the community. He says that a theologian attempts to "catch up what Christianity is basically all about in a single, synoptic, imaginative judgment."[22]

Now, at great risk of oversimplification, I'm suggesting that the adoption of a dualist anthropology in the early centuries of the church was largely responsible for changing Christians' conception of what Christianity is basically all about. A more nuanced account would involve the contributions of Neoplatonism as a whole, interacting with Constantinianism, but time and my lack of knowledge of church history prevent me from giving a thorough analysis.

One simple and obvious example of the way dualism allowed Christians to change the subject concerns the doctrine of salvation. The New Testament conception of participating in a partially realized Kingdom of God while awaiting its coming in full has lost out to an emphasis on saving individual souls for a transcendent heaven.

For another example, consider Christology. Both Yoder and McClendon contest typical metaphysical interpretations of the hymn to Christ in Philippians 2. In the nineteenth century it was taken to speak of a heavenly being who emptied himself, the pre-incarnate Christ, who divested himself of the "form" of God in order to take on human form. In accordance with the long theological tradition's conception of the attributes of God, that of which the Son emptied himself was his omnipotence, omnipresence, and omniscience. McClendon (along with many others) argues that this interpretation of the hymn reads later concerns back into Paul's letter. Paul's real concern can best be perceived by the way he uses the hymn to parallel, with regard to Christ, a point he makes about himself in the following chapter: he counts as rubbish all the prerogatives he has renounced for Christ's sake – his race, his tribe, being of the right school of thought, and exhibiting impeccable zeal (Phil. 3:5-10). Both cases, Christ's emptying himself and Paul's renunciation of high social status, are presented as models for the Philippians, who are to empty themselves of "selfish ambition and vanity" (Phil. 2:3).

Thus, McClendon argues that Jesus' decision not to grasp after "the form of God" means in this context that he rejected, not metaphysical perfections, but the very earthly temptations to kingship in favor of identification with servants and outcasts, even though that identification would lead to his death.

Noting that the incarnational theology of the Bible translators has affected their rendering of the Greek, McClendon offers his own translation as follows:

Take to heart among yourselves your being in Christ Jesus: who, mirroring God *on earth,* turned back the temptation to rival God and poured out his life, taking a servant role. Bearing the likeness of *Adam's* race, sharing the human lot, he brought his life low, obedient to death (death by a cross).[23]

Yoder relates the passage to Paul's interpretation of Christ as the new Adam, and reaches a conclusion similar to McClendon's. "Being in God's likeness" does not mean being God. Eve and Adam were made in God's likeness, but were tempted to grasp at a more lofty godlikeness – the root act of rebellion.[24]

So here is a socio-political rather than metaphysical reading of Jesus' kenosis, and it supports the claim that to be made in God's image has to do not with possession of an immortal, immaterial soul, but rather with costly obedience.

So why should Mennonites and Brethren be interested in a nonreductive physicalist account of human nature? In short, it deprives Christians of what has provided eighteen centuries of believers with a distraction from doing the work of Jesus, peacefully, simply, together.

II.
God's Nonviolent Direct Action

Nancey Murphy
April 7, 2001

1. Introduction

It's always a pleasure for me to speak at a Mennonite institution, especially when the topic is peace. It's ironic that at most other places, even Christian places, talking about peace and nonviolence is a good way to provoke a heated argument. When Christians argue about nonviolence, their differences usually come down to differences in how they understand the moral authority of Jesus. Some Christians say that all ethical teaching needs to be based on the life and teaching of Jesus. Others say that Jesus' teaching is valuable for some issues but not sufficient. In addition you have to look for God's will expressed in creation, and you do this by observing how God has ordered the natural world. These theorists can then say: yes, Jesus taught nonviolence, turning the other cheek, but that doesn't mean that there are no legitimate uses of violence. For example, Romans 13 says that government authority was ordained by God, it is part of God's creation, and therefore Christians may have a duty to defend the state by violence.

My plan in this lecture is to present an argument for nonviolence, and to do that I'm going to turn arguments from the so-called "orders of creation" on their heads. I'm going to argue that what we see in nature is the same kind of nonviolent divine action that we see in Jesus.

2. An Analogy

To describe the structure of my argument I begin with an image. Consider a ladder. A ladder has two upright pieces, and they are held

29

together by the rungs. I'm going to present two accounts of God's action: one of how God interacts with us, his human creatures; and one of how God acts in the natural world. Think of these two accounts as the uprights of the ladder. To connect the two – to form the rungs – I'll describe points of similarity or analogy between the two accounts. I'll begin with an account of God's dealing with humans, and this will be quite unoriginal and uncontentious. However, my account of God's action in the natural world will be more original, more speculative, and therefore more open to challenge.

2.1 God's Action in the Human World

For my account of God's action in the human world I am following a lovely book by Daniel Day Williams, titled *The Spirit and the Forms of Love*.[25] As the title suggests, this is a book about love in its many forms, and about its relation to the work of God's Spirit. Williams argues that the concept of love has a history, and as we pursue that history through the development of Hebrew and Christian thought, the character of God's activity comes more clearly into focus.

Williams says that there are two contrasting tendencies in Hebrew thought regarding the character of divine action. One tendency is to interpret the action of God primarily in terms of divine *power*: In this line of thought, the prophet looks forward to "the sheer assertion of the divine majesty in an act which restores the whole earth to its rightful obedience to the divine order"; "the righteous God will do what he will do" (p. 28).

The second tendency interprets God's action in terms of the renewal of the marriage bond between God and Israel. But this requires a transformation of the heart. This *relational* view of divine action stresses God's mercy and faithfulness, and begins to suggest that redemption is a costly act for God: "[God's] power remains sovereign, and its work will be done, but God does not live untouched by what happens" (p. 33).

When we get to the New Testament, this second tendency comes to the fore. The love between God and Jesus presents the ideal love, from which the human race continually falls short. "God has to deal with a humanity" says Williams, "which can learn to love and be reached by love only through the divine self-giving and suffering. . . . The character of the divine love is shown by Jesus' obedience . . . and his giving of himself for all. . . . [s]uffering love poured out for another beyond the worthiness of the other" (pp. 37-38).

Williams then surveys major conceptions of love in later Christian thought: for example, the evangelical Protestant conception of love as grace, and Francis of Assisi's conception of love as renunciation of self and as unpretentious service of others, free from attachments to privilege and power. This survey leads to an analysis of what Williams calls the structure of love, and this in turn serves as a framework for understanding God's action. The requirements of love include the following:

First, individuality: Love requires real individuals – it does not destroy the uniqueness of the one who is loved.

Second, it requires freedom: The response of the beloved cannot be bought or coerced; therefore to love is to risk, since the beloved may choose not to respond in kind.

Third, suffering: To love is to act, but it is also to be acted upon. Thus to love is to have one's freedom circumscribed by the other; it is to accept the inevitability of being conformed to the other.

Williams concludes from his list of love's requirements that divine action in the human sphere cannot be understood as the exercise of sheer power; God's power is not absolute omnipotence, but rather the power to do everything that is consistent with love. God's love subjects God to the suffering, which follows upon the creature's freedom. God acts by means of a suffering love that leaves its object free to respond in kind or to refuse. God's love does not end all risk, but accepts every risk that is necessary for its work. God does not resolve every conflict, but accepts conflict as the arena in which the work of love is to be done. God does not neatly separate the good from the bad, but seeks the reconciliation of every life so that it may share with all the others (pp. 137-38).

Humankind, created in God's image, is created to participate in God's creativity, in its splendor and its suffering (p. 135).

2.2 God's Action in the Natural World

God's action in the natural world is one of the modern period's most significant theological problems. It has affected Scriptural interpretation and doctrine. It has contributed to atheism, and it has helped to drive a wedge between liberal and conservative Christians.[26] To a great extent, it has been modern science that has caused the problem. As we have come to recognize the lawlike behavior of natural entities, we have found it increasingly difficult to reconcile divine action with natural causation.[27]

I'll classify modern positions on divine action under three headings: deism, interventionism, and immanentism. The deist says that God's activity is limited to the initial creation of the universe, which includes the establishment of the laws that will govern its behavior. I'll not spend time on this option, because it is simply not compatible with a Christian view of God, who is not only Creator, but also Redeemer, Revealer, and Provider.

The interventionist understands God's continuing action in the world as – intervention. That is, at specific times and places, God causes events to occur that are different from what would have occurred if God had not acted. In other words, God interferes with the natural processes, overrides natural causes to impose the divine will on the created order.

Interventionists vary widely in their views of the degree or frequency of God's intervention. For some, God acts constantly in day-to-day life, bringing about small miracles here and there, often in answer to prayer. For others, God's interventions are restricted to the great events of the biblical drama, such as the special creation of the human species, the Exodus, the Incarnation and Resurrection.

The immanentist says, in contrast, that if God works in the universe at all – if any event is a divine act – then it only makes sense to suppose that every event is in some sense an act of God. So God acts "immanently" in and through the processes of nature and history. The long history of the universe is one magnificent, creative act of God.[28]

A range of views is possible here also, bounded on one end by the view that God's involvement amounts merely to approval of events determined by natural laws, and bounded on the other by the view that all events are such direct enactments of God's intentions that natural causation is finally illusory. This latter view has been called occasionalism; we might label the former the "rubber stamp" view. When I say that the range is bounded by these two views, I mean that neither is acceptable, and the theologian's job is to try to stake out a position somewhere between occasionalism and conceding that God does nothing but rubber stamp the natural order. This turns out to be exceedingly difficult, though.

While a respect for modern science does not strictly require an immanentist account of divine action, it is clear that science has pushed theologians in that direction. The first major step was the development of the Newtonian account of planetary motion. Medieval cosmology had placed the heavenly bodies under the control of the angels, but with Newton's application of the laws of motion, a purely mechanical account could be given. This clockwork universe provided the primary motivation for deism as well as for immanentism.

Another important contribution to this process came from the theory of evolution. In fact, much of the opposition to evolutionary theory on the part of highly conservative Christians can be understood as a reaction to claims that the appearance, first of life and then of human beings, requires no special divine creative acts – no interventions in the natural order.

Now, if we interpret these scientific advances as steps in a cumulative argument against an interventionist view of divine action, there is now a further step. Interestingly, it is one that interrelates biological evolution and physical cosmology. The developments I refer to are calculations regarding the so-called fine-tuning of the basic features of the universe in such a way as to make it capable, against tremendous odds, of sustaining life.

It is easy to imagine universes where life would not be possible. Cosmologist George Ellis writes:

> There could be a universe that expanded and then recollapsed
> with a total lifetime of only one hundred thousand years;

evolution could not take place on that timescale. The background radiation might never drop below three thousand K, so that matter would always have been ionized (electrons and nuclei always remaining separate from each other); the molecules of life could then never form. Black holes might [have been] so common that they rapidly attracted all the matter in the universe, and there never would have been a stable environment in which life could develop. Cosmic rays could always be so abundant that any tentative organic structures would be destroyed before they could replicate.

There are many ways in which the boundary conditions in a universe could prevent life occurring. But additionally, we can conceive of universes where the laws of physics (and so of chemistry) were different [from] ours. Almost any change in these laws will prevent life as we know it from functioning. If the neutron mass were just a little less than it is, proton decay could have taken place so that no atoms were left at all. The production of carbon and oxygen in stars requires the careful setting of two different nuclear energy levels; if they were just a little different, the elements we need for life would not exist. Perhaps most important of all, the chemistry on which the human body depends involves intricate folding and bonding patterns that would be destroyed if the fine structure constant (which controls the nature of chemical bonding) were a little bit different.[29]

So if initial conditions, such as the total mass of the universe or any of the basic numbers, such as the strength of the gravitational constant, had been off even by a tiny fraction, the universe would have evolved differently and there could be no life of any sort.

Now, what bearing do these calculations have on an understanding of divine action? One conclusion is that the conditions for life and intelligence (and thus for the emergence of creatures with free will) were built into the universe at the very beginning. While this does not preclude God's special creation of life in general or of human beings, it makes such a view extremely implausible. God's *regular* way of working seems to be to build into the system from the beginning all that is needed for its later development. In cosmologists' terms, the universe is *anthropic:* the potential for human observers was present in the universe from the beginning. In theological terms, God has made "created co-creators": entities that participate in the ongoing development of higher forms of being.[30] None of this, as I say, proves that an interventionist account of divine action is impossible. Yet I myself have been much impressed by these results as evidence to the effect that God works *through* created structures and processes, not by interrupting or overriding them.

If we reject an interventionist account of divine action, we are left with two options: either God does not act at all within the created world, or else God acts at all times in all things. I have already suggested that Christians must rule out deism; this leaves immanentism – the view that God acts in all events.

However, I have also suggested that there are two extreme positions that the immanentist must avoid: The rubber stamp view of God as merely supporting and approving the natural processes is functionally equivalent to deism, in that we lose any sense of God's directing the process, and of any special acts of divine providence. However, occasionalism is also unacceptable in that it denies the "functional integrity"[31] of creation – it makes natural causation an illusion. It has the further disadvantage of making God entirely and directly responsible for all evil and suffering. How shall we steer between these two extremes? My plan is to present an account of God's action in the natural world that is consistent with current science and that also bears striking analogies to the account given above of God's action in the human world. It will turn out that this account does indeed avoid the pitfalls just mentioned.

What are the essential features of our account of divine action in the human realm? In light of Williams's work I suggested three:

First, God creates genuine individuals, with his or her own integrity, created power, capacities, and typical behavior – that is, his or her own created power to participate in creation.

Second, God respects human freedom. God cooperates with, but does not overpower, the creature.

And third, God accepts the cost of respecting the individuality and freedom of human creatures. This means that God's control of any particular event is limited; suffering and evil cannot always be prevented.

I want to suggest, now, that God's action in the natural world is entirely analogous. First, it is important to note that if God is to act in all events and entities, then God must act in the most elementary constituents of the universe, since these are among the entities that exist in the world. So it is reasonable to suppose that God's primary mode of action within complex entities is by means of action within their most basic constituents. Thus, my proposal is that God acts in all things by acting within the smallest constituent parts of the universe. According to contemporary science, these are subatomic "particles" such as quarks and electrons.[32] The interesting feature of these entities, for present purposes, is the *indeterminacy* of their behavior. While indeterminacy and free will are not the same thing, indeterminacy will provide a valuable analogue for free will in an account of divine action.

So the analogies with our account of God's dealings with humans are as follows:

First, God has created a universe which, at this point in its history, is made up of individuals, howsoever small and ephemeral. These subatomic entities have built-in capacities – types of behavior specific to their own kinds.

Second, while the possible range of such an entity's behavior is given by the kind of particle it is, the *when* is undetermined. Thus God can act upon it, causing it to do what it does *now* rather than at another time, without overpowering it in any sense. There is room for God's cooperation with the natural capacities of these entities.

But, third, this is a *costly* withholding of God's power, since it means that God's scope for determining natural events is limited by respect for the integrity of these tiny creatures.

It is an extremely complex issue to try to say what this theory of divine action actually "permits" God to do. It is beyond our computational powers to describe the myriad quantum-level events that would have to be coordinated to bring about an event in the macroscopic world. Also, many have argued against an account of divine action based at the quantum level, on the grounds that any effect God might have at this level would be averaged out at the macroscopic level, since quantum events obey statistical laws in the aggregate. However, I see no need to assume that God must always be restricted by these statistical averages.[33]

John Polkinghorne, in his discussion of the problem of evil, has suggested that just as we need a free will defense in order to understand God's permitting of moral evil. Similarly, we need a "free process defense" in order to understand God's permitting of natural disasters and suffering.[34] The account presented here is much indebted to this suggestion. God *is* acting in all created entities and events, and truly affecting the course of those processes, yet the scope of God's activity is constrained by God's free choice to respect the freedom and integrity of creatures, all the way from electrons to humans. God is neither a passive approver of all that happens, nor solely responsible for every outcome.

Williams has emphasized the costliness to God of God's decision to cooperate with human creatures rather than to overrule them by sheer power. Holmes Rolston has extended this insight to the world of nature. Rolston's thesis is that suffering in the natural world is, in a sense, redemptive. It is a necessary by-product of the features of life that allow for the emergence of something higher. And just as God suffers in and with human suffering to bring forth greater good, God suffers, as well, in and with all of life. I quote Rolston's beautiful prose at length:

> The Earth is a divine creation and scene of providence. The whole natural history is somehow contained in God, God's doing, and that includes even suffering, which, if it is difficult to say simply that it is immediately from God, is not ultimately outside of God's plan and redemptive control. God absorbs suffering and transforms it into goodness. . . .
>
> [N]ature is . . . *cruciform*. The world is not a paradise of hedonistic ease, but a theater where life is learned and earned by labor, a drama where even the evils drive us to make sense

of things. Life is advanced not only by thought and action, but by suffering; not only by logic but by pathos. . . .

This pathetic element in nature is seen in faith to be at the deepest logical level the pathos in God. God is not in a simple way the Benevolent Architect, but is rather the Suffering Redeemer. The whole of the earthen metabolism needs to be understood as having this character. The God met in physics as the divine wellspring from which matter-energy bubbles up . . . is in biology the suffering and resurrecting power that redeems life out of chaos. . . .

The secret of life is seen now to lie not so much in the heredity molecules, not so much in natural selection and the survival of the fittest, not so much in life's informational, cybernetic learning. The secret of life is that it is a passion play. Things perish in tragedy. The religions knew that full well, before biology arose to reconfirm it. But things perish with a passing over in which the sacrificed individual also flows in the river of life. Each of the suffering creatures is delivered over as an innocent sacrificed to preserve a line, a blood sacrifice perishing that others may live. We have a kind of "slaughter of the innocents," a nonmoral, naturalistic harbinger of the slaughter of the innocents at the birth of the Christ, all perhaps vignettes hinting of the innocent lamb slain from the foundation of the world. They share the labor of the divinity. In their lives, beautiful, tragic, and perpetually incomplete, they speak for God; they prophesy as they participate in the divine pathos. All have "borne our griefs and carried our sorrows."

The abundant life that Jesus exemplifies and offers to his disciples is that of a sacrificial suffering through to something higher. There is something divine about the power to suffer through to something higher. The Spirit of God is the genius that makes alive, that redeems life from its evils. The cruciform creation is, in the end, deiform, godly, just because of this element of struggle, not in spite of it. There is a great divine "yes" hidden behind and within every "no" of crushing nature. God, who is the lure toward rationality and sentience in the upcurrents of the biological pyramid, is also the compassionate lure in, with, and under all purchasing of life at the cost of sacrifice. God rescues from suffering, but the Judeo-Christian faith never teaches that God eschews suffering in the achievement of the divine purposes. To the contrary, seen in the paradigm of the cross, God too suffers, not less than his creatures, in order to gain for his creatures a more abundant life.[35]

3. Our Response

Rolston has already hinted that the disciples of such a God as this must join in *suffering-through* to something higher. So let us turn now to the question with which we began, that of the relation of a creation ethic to the ethical teaching and example of Jesus. The contrast, of course, is between an ethic of nonviolence and an ethic that permits violent coercion. There are a variety of arguments used to legitimate warfare and violent self-defense, and many of them turn on the notion that we can learn about God's will for our lives by observing how God has ordered the created universe. In particular, Romans 13 states that governmental authority has been *ordained by God* – it is a part of God's creative providence for human life. Therefore, Christians have an overriding duty to obey and defend the state, even by force of arms, if necessary.

However, I contend that if we wish to take our moral cues from creation, we must not look at the *structures* that have been created, since, on the theory of divine action presented here, all created structures must be viewed as joint effects of the divine will and of the wills of created co-creators. In short, the institutions of society are not pure expressions or reflections of the will of God.

Where, then, do we look for moral guidance? I suggest that we look not at the *products* of divine creative action, but rather at the *moral character* of that action. And, in fact, this has been the burden of the first part of this lecture. The moral character of God's action includes constant *involvement* – not a distant deistic indifference. It includes *respect* for the integrity and freedom of created entities, striving to bring them to perfection by cooperation, not by force. It accepts the *cost* of that withholding of power – the inefficiency and waste, even the suffering.

Now, you can surely see where my argument is headed. I am prepared to claim that an ethic of creation *is* an ethic of nonviolence. That is, nonviolence in the arena of interpersonal and social conflict reflects the moral qualities of God's own action.

There are a variety of ways of being nonviolent. I'll concentrate here on "nonviolent resistance," the deliberate refusal to respond in kind to violent attack. The term "resistance" highlights the fact that it is not mere acquiescence, but rather is aimed at stopping abuse and changing the situation exactly by refusing to retaliate.

But the goal is not merely to stop the attack. The attack provides an opportunity to show respect for the attacker in a dramatic way by refusing to retaliate. This show of respect is intended to allow or provoke the aggressor's better motives to come to the fore in the hope of reconciliation.

Romano Guardini writes that:

> Everything, to remain human and be spiritually successful, must first pass through the "personal center," that inmost core of the responsible human heart. The true, the good and the right are realizable only if accepted by living people with inner, genuine conviction, and to bring this about requires reverence, encouragement, patience. He who would be truly effective with men must respect *their* freedom, stir *their* initiatives, awaken *their* creative centers.[36]

So nonviolent resistance is a way to resist evil and work for the betterment of society by cooperation and reconciliation, not by coercion. Such action shows respect for the individuals involved, especially those with whom one is in conflict, by refusing to attack them. It is persuasive, aiming to elicit and cooperate with the best in others. Finally, it accepts the cost: costs in the form of reduced effectiveness, of lack of control, and especially of physical suffering. The parallels here with the previous account of divine action are obvious: God's constant involvement for good in the natural and human worlds, God's withholding of coercive power out of respect for the integrity and freedom of all created individuals, and God's willingness to bear the cost of that lack of coercive control.

I said a moment ago that one of the costs of a nonviolent approach to social action is that it may be less effective than coercion. Is this the case, and if so, does speaking of God's nonviolent action imply that God is ineffective? If we look at circumscribed consequences of nonviolent action, it often appears that it is less effective than the use of force would have been. However, I believe the Anabaptists had an important insight to offer here: a result gained by force is not the same result, however much it may resemble it superficially, as a result gained by free and intelligent cooperation.

4. Conclusion

In concluding, I ask you to reflect with me on the value of the argument I have presented here. I acknowledge that my account of God's action in the natural world is not the only possible interpretation of the scientific results. For example, it has been more common to identify God as the creator of a nature "red in tooth and claw." And, as you all know, nonviolence is a controversial position in Christian circles. So why should anyone who is not already a convinced pacifist accept my argument?

The first answer is consistency: I have presented a view of divine action wherein Jesus' "suffering through to something higher" is the paradigm of all of God's interaction with creation, not a shocking exception; and where the disciples' action takes on the same cruciform pattern.

But maybe there are other consistent accounts – a triumphalist view of Christ's death, for instance, as paradigm for the rule of a magnificent earthly church.

It's not possible to defend my account against all possible competitors here, but I can take one further step toward its justification. I do so by pointing out the advantages of a view such as mine for answering the problem of evil. This is the problem of why evil and suffering are permitted by an omnipotent and all-loving God. Answers to this problem often begin with the assumption that God has some sufficient reason for permitting the evils and suffering we observe. In the case of moral evil or sin, the traditional answer for centuries has been that it is a necessary consequence of human freedom. God counts it worth the cost of sin to have creatures who respond freely to divine love. Augustine, an early proponent of this view, argued that all forms of natural evil and suffering could be accounted for on this basis as well: sickness, natural disasters, and even death, are consequences of, or punishment for, sin.

Augustine's account of natural evil is no longer universally accepted. It is clear that animals suffered and died for aeons before humans and human sinfulness appeared on the scene. Many, also, struggle pastorally with an Augustinian view of suffering as the wages of sin – for they see too many cases of terrible suffering falling disproportionately upon the innocent.

The view of divine action presented here makes an important contribution to answering this question. It assumes that God is working at all times in all things to bring about the good, but the extent to which God can realize those good plans is, by divine decree, dependent upon the cooperation of all-too-often-recalcitrant creatures, both human and non-human. As well, a universe in which creatures, however slowly and painfully, come to cooperate freely with the divine plan is incomparably better than one that is simply a manifestation of God's power. Diogenes Allen puts it this way:

> When God creates, it means that he allows something to exist which is not himself. This requires an act of profound renunciation. He chooses out of love to permit something else to exist, something created to be itself and to exist by virtue of its own interest and value. So the creation of a world means

that God renounces his status as the only existent – he pulls himself back, so to speak, in order to give his creation room to exist for its own sake.[37]

God's voluntary withholding permits things genuinely other than God to exist, but only God has God's perfections. So in the natural world, in the process of evolution, for instance, we see emerging, slowly over the course of time, creatures in God's image. Yet along the way, the recalcitrant process is slow, wasteful, inefficient, painful. In the human world God has revealed a plan for our lives that will bring peace, joy, and fulfillment, yet we squander our years in painful rebellion.

Yet, if the death of Jesus is the ultimate act of God's withholding of power, then Jesus' resurrection is the promise and foretaste of final victory. The apparent ineffectiveness of God's suffering love must be judged in light of this unexpected and total transformation. It is an outcome that cannot be forced or seized by violence.

III.
Evolution: One Anabaptist's Perspective

By Nancey Murphy
April 8, 2001

1. Introduction

My topic is Christianity and evolution. My addressing this issue reflects
something of a conversion in my life. When I first became involved with
the science-religion dialogue I shied away from the evolution issue partly
because it is so contentious but also because I thought that it was not an
intellectually interesting issue – all of the important intellectual moves
had already been made at least several generations ago. However, I have
a friend who is a professor of biology at the University of California and
who teaches a thousand freshmen each year. He estimates that ninety
percent of his students come to class believing that they cannot both
hold to their religious beliefs and also accept what he is trying to teach
them. Since most of the students are pre-med majors, they take a lot of
biology in four years and become convinced of the scientific evidence.
What happens, then, to their religious convictions? Some manage to put
religion in one pocket and science in the other, but many of them simply
give up their church commitments. So I felt a calling at that point to
make this issue one of my own, especially since I teach in a seminary.
Many of my students will be pastors in the sorts of churches where
evolution is an issue. Thus, I feel I have a duty to deal with the issue in
class as often as curriculum permits and also to try to encourage my
colleagues to do likewise.

I don't expect that there is any "missionary work" involved in
addressing this audience. However, I hope that I can say a few things

about the controversies that are not already obvious to you. Then I'll comment on how I see the evolution issue to connect with Anabaptist thinking.

My plan is, first, to give a brief overview of the types of responses Christians have made to evolution. These are organized in terms of the degree of acceptance of evolutionary biology. They are not organized historically because there has been a spectrum of responses to evolutionary biology ever since it came into existence. Next I'll suggest that much of what is involved in the controversy is actually a controversy about the nature of divine action.[38] Finally, I'll turn to the ethical issues related to evolutionary biology. This will force me to look at the context in which evolutionary biology grew up, and I'll end by considering the relations among natural theology, Darwin's theory, and conservative social agendas.

2. Types of Responses to Darwin

There have been a vast array of responses to evolutionary biology, but they are often grouped into types in order to give an overview. Again, this is in order of increasing acceptance of evolutionary biology. The first type is that of the Young Earth, or Six-Day Creationists. These take the Genesis account literally, including the claim that when the story says "day," it means an actual twenty-four-hour period.

Close kin are the Old Earth Creationists. These theorists have done some work to try to harmonize a literal reading of the creation story with the old age of the earth by saying that a day does not mean literally twenty-four hours, but is used to refer to an aeon. So creation happens just as the story says, but it is spread out in time, sometimes perhaps with billions of years between one creation event and another.

The third is type of position is Progressive Creationism. According to this view, much of the development of the universe happens according to natural laws, but there are specific creative acts of God that occur in the process. Creation of life itself would be one of those special creative events; creation of human beings would be another. There is a spectrum of views on how many additional interventions are needed – for example, depending on whether a special act of creation is needed for each species. This position represents an important shift from the two previous views in that it no longer sees a need for reading the creation stories literally.

The fourth view is Theistic Evolution. This is the view that God creates *through* the evolutionary process, and so it accepts the scientific account of how evolution happens, but claims simply that it is God's means of creation. I believe it is necessary to distinguish two sub-types here. On the one hand, there are those who say that the evolutionary process is guided by God (and this comes close to progressive creationism if it is guided by specific interventions). On the other, there are those who say that God simply creates a universe in which evolution will take place, and the evolutionary process itself, without any divine guidance, serves God's purposes in creating life and human beings.

The fifth possibility is what Ian Barbour calls the Two-Worlds Approach to science and religion.[39] This view is typical of classic liberal Protestant theology, according to which theology and science are essentially concerned with such different matters that there is no need to try to harmonize them at any point. Therefore, whatever science teaches about origins is true from a scientific point of view and not relevant to theology.

These approaches have been available throughout the history of Christian responses to evolutionary theory. It is important, in addition, to mention two very powerful movements in recent history. The first of these is the Creation Science movement. This movement is about 30 years old and, interestingly enough, is in part a consequence of the cold war. Sputnik went up; the U.S. government put emphasis on the teaching of science in the public schools. New biology textbooks were written that gave prominent place to evolutionary theory. In response there was an attempt to get creation taught as an alternative theory in the public school classrooms. Teaching creation itself was ruled unconstitutional because it is religion, and so the creation science movement arose as an attempt to argue that there is an alternative *scientific* account of the origins of life and humankind. It has been backed by attempts to find empirical evidence, especially evidence supporting the young age of the earth.

More recent, and much more prominent on the intellectual scene, is the Intelligent Design movement. This movement began about ten years ago with the publication of Phillip Johnson's book, *Darwin on Trial.*[40] This is a much more sophisticated movement and, again, is an attempt to get an alternative view regarding origins accepted in the public school curriculum. Johnson, Michael Behe, and William Dembski are most prominent in the movement. These three attempt to show, in one way or another, that evolutionary biology is not an adequate account of origins, and therefore needs to be supplemented by an alternative point of view, which is intelligent design. They tend to say little about their positive views on origins, but because Johnson rejects the claim that one species can evolve from another, whether he claims the title or not, he can be classified as a progressive creationist.

What has struck me about this controversy is that it is really a controversy about how God acts. When one asks the question of how something comes into being there tends to be, for those who oppose evolutionary theory, an opposition between divine action and natural processes. Creation happens *exclusively* by means of divine action for both the Young Earth and the Old Earth creationists. Progressive Creationists say that the present state of the universe is a result of natural processes *and* divine action, but here I need to make a distinction. The progressive creationists attribute *some* developments to natural processes and *others* to divine action – it is an either/or relationship. The difference between this position and the theistic evolutionists is dramatic because the theistic evolutionists say that *every* development is a result of natural processes *along with* divine action.

In a somewhat different sense, the two-worlds theorists would say the same thing. Natural processes serve to explain events as long as one looks at them from the scientific side, yet everything that happens is a part of God's providential ordering. So again we have natural processes plus divine action. The critical difference, then, is whether one sees divine action to be opposed to natural processes, or whether one sees divine action as always occurring in and through natural processes.[41]

Those of us in theological education ought not to be criticizing the Creationist and Intelligent Design movements by trying to present arguments for the truth of evolutionary biology, which few of us are equipped to do. What we should be criticizing is their theory of divine action. The Christian tradition has always maintained that everything that happens is in some sense divine action, and then has also often countenanced special divine acts or miracles in addition. Creationist positions tend to leave out of account God's normal, regular way of working and to focus strictly on what we would call the miraculous or the special divine acts. This is a deeply defective understanding of God's relationship to the world, making God and natural causes competitors in determining the outcome of creaturely processes.

I am also critical of two-worlds theologians who say that science and religion have nothing to do with one another, and that therefore theologians have no need to address biological issues *at all*. It is not that science and religion are giving competing accounts of how things came to be, but rather that there is a very serious question that biology raises, especially as interpreted by some of its atheistic proponents, about the character of the God who would create through a process like evolution. I'll return to this issue shortly.

Robert Pennock, in his recent book, *Tower of Babel*, provides an instructive overview of the Intelligent Design movement, along with critiques of some of their more sophisticated arguments.[42] What I found most interesting was his consideration of the moral motivation behind Johnson's work. Johnson's second book, *Reason in the Balance*, has in the first chapter about twenty references to male and female sex roles, family, monogamy, and sexual behavior.[43] Pennock's conclusion is that this illustrates a major motivation for the campaign against evolutionary biology – the belief that it undermines "traditional family values."

3. Ethics and Evolution

Having raised the issue of the relationship between evolution and ethics, I want to shift from criticism to a consideration of what I think the real issues ought to be for Christians as they think about evolutionary biology. The anti-evolutionists are not wrong to ask about the relation between evolution and ethics, but I disagree with them about the particular ethical issues that are involved. I recently studied the history of the development of evolutionary biology with the intention of writing a critique of the social ethic called Social Darwinism that is taken to be based on evolutionary biology – laissez-faire economics, survival of the economically fittest, and justification for failure to assist the poor. I was quite surprised to find that after Darwin produced his biological works there were a variety of uses made of his theory to support social programs – not just the conservative program that we think as Social Darwinism; it was used by socialists and by liberals as well.

I was also surprised by the history because, whereas I understood "Social Darwinism" to have been a *result* of the development of Darwin's theory, the historical causation is at least as much the reverse. Attitudes toward the poor that were prevalent during Darwin's day in fact helped to create Darwin's understanding of biology. Evolutionary theory grew out of a mixture of natural theology, Malthusian population theory, Darwin's observations, and the preceding history of the development of evolutionary ideas. All of these ingredients influenced Darwin's theory of natural selection.

Darwin was much influenced by the work of William Paley and his design argument. Paley's work conditioned Darwin and others in his day to see features of nature as specifically and intentionally designed by God. So Darwin was predisposed to read the character, the intentions, and the activities of God off of the characteristics of the natural world.

A second ingredient in Darwin's thinking is found in the work of Thomas Malthus, in his *Essay on the Principle of Population* (1798). The principle of population states that population, if unchecked, will grow geometrically whereas food supply will increase, at most, arithmetically. Thus, struggle, competition, and starvation are the natural result. Malthus's principle of population was the key to Darwin's thinking. It had already been proposed that species could change into others; already the old age of the earth had been established by the geologists. So what was missing was the mechanism to get from one species to another.

Darwin came to the conclusion that selection was the principle of change from the study of domesticated animals. Then, reading Malthus, he saw how to extend this principle to the natural world: animals breed without "the moral restraint which in some small degree checks the increase in mankind."[44] Therefore, "the pressure is always ready. . . . A thousand wedges are being forced into the economy of nature. . . . The final cause of all this wedging must be to sort out proper structure and adapt it to change."[45] So Darwin concluded that it is the competition for food that produces the mechanism of change.

It is important to note that Malthus was an Anglican clergyman, who was working in the tradition of eighteenth-century natural theology. So his writings were not simply a scientific treatise on population growth and food supply, but rather they were, in a sense, a *theodicy* – an attempt to reconcile the goodness of God with evil and suffering. In place of Paley's "myriads of happy beings" Malthus sees struggle, inequality, suffering and death as the basic features of the natural world. And these are interpreted by him as the result of divine providence. So Paley had set everyone up to say that, whatever the character of the natural order is, God made it. Malthus's role was to say that the character of the natural world is starvation and dog eat dog. This, then, reflects on God's intentions and it is also seen as providential. Malthus wrote that evil produces exertion, exertion produces mind, and mind produces progress. So in the end it is *good* that there is not enough food to go around.

The difference between eighteenth-century political and economic views and those after Malthus was the loss of optimism. The limits placed on economic growth by the limits on food production meant that the growing population of urban poor was seen in terms of surplus mouths, rather than as an economically beneficial surplus of labor. Thus, Malthus and his followers argued that relief to the poor should be restricted, since it only postponed the collapse of those who could not support themselves. Malthus argued that a law should be passed such that no child born from any marriage more than a year after the law was passed should be entitled to parish assistance. After Malthus it was not uncommon for other theologians to take up the cause. Thomas Chalmers, professor of divinity at the University of Edinburgh emphasized the necessity of moral restraint, especially sexual restraint, if the poor were to avoid the miseries to which the principle of population would lead. The necessary connection between moral weakness and misery was a reflection of the very character of God. Chalmers wrote:

> It is not the lesson of conscience, that God would, under the mere impulse of parental fondness for the creatures whom He has made, let down the high state and sovereignty which belong to Him; or that He would forebear the infliction of the penalty, because of any soft or timid shrinking from the pain it would give the objects of His displeasure. . . . [W]hen one looks to the disease and the agony of spirit, and above all the hideous and unsparing death, with its painful struggles and gloomy forebodings, which are spread universally over the face of the earth – we cannot but imagine of the God who presides over such an economy, that He is not a being who will falter from the imposition of his severity, which might serve the objects of a high administration.[46]

So, a rather gloomy view of God and God's purposes! The question then is what role Darwinian theory actually played in the development of Social Darwinism. Historian Robert Young says that all Darwin's theory actually did was to provide a simple change in the source of the justification for social stratification. Now the basis of social stratification among rich and poor changes from a theological theodicy to a biological one in which the so-called physiological division of labor provides a scientific guarantee of the rightness of the property and work relations of industrial society. . . .

> The famous controversy in the nineteenth century between science and theology was very heated indeed, and scholars have concentrated on this level of analysis. However, at another level, the protagonists in the debate were in fundamental agreement. They were fighting over the best ways of rationalizing the same set of assumptions about the existing order. An explicitly theological theodicy was being challenged by a secular one based on biological conceptions and the fundamental assumption of the uniformity of nature.[47]

So the theological context in which Darwin's theory was developed was largely responsible for the conflictual imagery in Darwin's language. It is not surprising, therefore, that his theory could be used to support the same social agenda as that which contributed to its development. Now this raises another question. If Darwin's perception of how nature works was influenced by thinkers such as Malthus and Chalmers, has this affected only his theory of natural selection, or has it affected his and subsequent scientists' perception of nature itself? I think that the latter is true, and this is an important point for theologians to recognize. Here I believe the two-worlds theologians are slightly inaccurate in saying that theologians do not need to deal with the theory of evolution. Darwin predisposes us, thanks to earlier theologians, to see nature as "red in tooth and claw," to perceive in nature only struggle and competition. The theological question is, what kind of a God sponsors this?

A number of people have challenged Christianity by asking: if God does create through the evolutionary process, why did he choose a process that has so much waste, so much suffering, and so much death? An important book for present purposes is Frans de Waal's *Good Natured*. This is a charming book, which takes issue with the impression we have had of the "moral" nature of nature since Darwin. He points out that there is a great deal of cooperation among animals. There is what we can scarcely refrain from calling caring behavior, a certain level of unconscious morality. Here is one of the more charming passages from de Waal's book.

> A British ethologist, Anne Rasa, followed the final days of a low ranking adult male [in a colony of dwarf mongoose] dying of chronic kidney disease. The male lived in a captive group consisting of a pair and its offspring. Two adjustments took place. First, the sick male was allowed to eat much earlier in the rank order than previously. . . . Second, the rest of the group changed from sleeping on elevated objects, such as boxes, to sleeping on the floor once the sick male had lost the ability to climb up onto the boxes. They stayed in contact

with him, grooming him much more than usual. After the male's death, the group slept with the cadaver until its decay made removal necessary.[48]

This is a very different picture of animal behavior than we get from the nature programs on television with their frequent portrayals of hunting and killing.

Noting that carnivores are usually taken to be the prime example of what nature is like, red in tooth and claw, he points out an interesting paradox. The animals that tend to have the most sociality, and consequently to care for one another the most, tend to be carnivores. This makes sense in evolutionary terms if you have a food source that is difficult to acquire, requires cooperation, and needs to be consumed rapidly before it spoils. So the animals that eat meat do tend to be the ones that develop sociality. De Waal speculates that much of the predisposition that humans have toward sociality was developed in ancestors that survived by carnivory.

Biology itself corrects the view of the evolutionary process as strikingly cruel and evil. Death is obviously necessary. First, there cannot be evolutionary progress without death of the earlier generation and without death of some members of the contemporary generation. To make this point vividly to my students, I ask if they would really like to have the dinosaurs around, all of them.

A related point: biology shows that it would probably not be possible to evolve creatures like ourselves, with our brain capacity and its huge need for nutrition, if animal species were all plant eaters. That is, vegetation alone cannot provide enough nutrition to get the kind of metabolism that is needed to support the large brains of the human species. Now, of course, we can be vegetarians, but this is because of our abundant food supply and our knowledge about how to balance amino acids. We probably could not have evolved as vegetarians.

Second, God is criticized as the designer of the evolutionary process because there are so many dead ends in the evolutionary tree. But why should species be immortal? What is supposed to be so terrible about there once having been dinosaurs and there not being dinosaurs anymore? This argument seems to me to be a red herring.

Pain is obviously necessary if there are to be organisms that exhibit complex behavior. Instinctual programming works for very, very simple organisms in a fairly simple environment. But if animals are to have the flexibility to behave in a variety of different ways and respond to a complex environment, then, in order simply to protect them from destroying themselves, they have to be able to feel pain.

My own view is that much of the rhetoric that paints the natural world in terms of evil and suffering is overblown. The chief exception to my view of good natured nature is cats, both house cats and big cats. They don't just kill to eat, but they play with their prey then, much later, eat it. Much as I love cats, I think that if God has anything to answer for it's those darn cats.

So, in short, if God is to create life, and this means real life, life that actually lives in its environment in an ecosystem and not just toy creatures that have to be kept alive by constant divine action, then the biological world has to be very much the way it is. Most of the suffering in nature (that is not caused by us) is *natural*; it simply needs to be present in order for there to be life at all, especially for there to be life like ourselves. Nonetheless, there is real suffering, and I refer you to Holmes Ralston's theological response to the suffering in nature.[49]

Another interesting theological perspective comes from the Anabaptist tradition. In radical-reformation thought the suffering of Christians is seen not so often as punishment for sin, but as costly participation with Christ in the likely consequences of obedience to God in the midst of a sinful world. Anabaptist leader Hans Hut proclaimed the Gospel of Christ crucified: "how he suffered for our sake and was obedient to the Father even unto death. In the same way we should walk after Christ, suffering for his sake all that is laid upon us, even unto death."[50] Several Anabaptist writers extended this account of human suffering to include the gospel of *all* creatures. Hut himself taught that the suffering of animals and the destruction of other living things conform to the pattern of redemption through suffering, and in its own way preaches the Gospel of Christ crucified. This suggests that the tendency to interpret the suffering in nature, as Rolston does, as a nonmoral harbinger of the suffering of Christ and his disciples, goes all the way back to the beginning of the Anabaptist tradition.

4. Conclusion

Although I did not intend my three lectures to be related, I was intrigued by the fact that the discussion of my first paper raised questions that were dealt with in my second paper, and the discussion of my second paper raised questions that were relevant to what I have said here. One way to sum up the connections is to say that I have argued that humans are essentially and fully a part of nature. Therefore, God's action in nature and God's action in human life are essentially one problem. The problem of divine action includes the scientific problem of how to reconcile it with our understanding of natural causation, but there is also the problem of evil. If God is constantly active in the world, then why do we see so little evidence of God's acting to prevent the suffering that comes as a consequence of natural processes? Proposing a theory of divine action in and through natural processes, that is, of God's cooperation with, rather than coercion or overriding of God's created entities, I have argued, is to propose an exhibition of God's moral character, which serves as a model of human behavior.

Discussions

The principal part of the conference consisted of discussions with Professor Murphy on the topics raised in her public and private lectures, as well as topics which arose naturally in the discussions themselves. The transcript of these discussions follows in a form adhering as closely as practicable to the original recorded discussions.

There are three main discussion sessions transcribed here. These are punctuated by the public and the internal lectures presented by Nancey Murphy. The discussions following the public lecture on Friday night were, regrettably, not recorded due to a communication problem. The Saturday morning discussions, Session I, do, however, refer to the Friday evening lecture.

In this transcript of the discussions the individual persons raising questions or providing comments are indicated by speaker numbers, as explained in the editor's preface. Professor Murphy is designated by name (Nancey Murphy). Both of these are given in bold-font. In certain instances it was impossible to identify the individual. In such instances the speaker number is replaced by the word "question" or "comment."

In some instances it was also impossible to distinguish the words. It was often possible, however, to distinguish the meaning of the speaker and, so, sentences could be completed. Conversational speech is also seldom grammatically perfect. Therefore, some liberty was taken in reforming sentences. Wherever possible the characteristics of the speaker were preserved, and every effort was made to preserve the ideas. As indicated in the editor's preface, these additions are in square brackets.

Effort was also made to keep the references to authors and texts referred to in the questions and comments. The editor takes full responsibility for all errors in these.

The discussion sessions are:

I.   Saturday Morning
II.   Saturday Afternoon
III.   Sunday Morning

I.
Saturday Morning

The Chair has outlined a procedure for orderly responses to Nancey and to the participants. New subjects and immediate comments will be distinguished by the participants' raising of a single pointing finger for a new subject or question, or the raising of a half or crooked finger for an immediate (short) comment on the present topic.

Nancey Murphy begins the discussion.

Nancey Murphy: Well, good morning. It's good to see you all again.

I am hoping that the session to some extent will be a discussion. I would like to invite you to reply to one another. Also, don't feel you have to make a question of whatever it is you have to say. That is, I would be happy to hear what you have to say on these issues as well.

Speaker 1: Historically, from what I know, a lot of discussion about the question of the existence of [the] soul revolves around the issue of free will. People arguing for the existence of a soul sort of underwrite that by arguing for the perceived need of having a free will as well. The question is, "How would your theory relate to that?" Perhaps there are theological reasons to say that the problem of free will is a red herring. Perhaps there are good reasons for neuroscience to say it is a red herring. How would you respond to that?

Nancey Murphy: As a matter of fact, I hope that my next book will be one that is jointly authored with Warren Brown, a colleague of mine from the school of psychology at Fuller [Theological Seminary]. We have been preparing to write such a book for a couple of years now. First of all, I want to distinguish between theological problems of free will and neuroscientific problems. I think that predestination or divine determination and neuroscience, that is the threat of neurobiological determinism, are entirely separate problems, even though in both cases the opposite of the problem we call free will. We believe that the determinism can be avoided, not by turning to indeterministic processes, as some people dealing with the neurosciences have done, because basically all that gives you is indeterminate action rather than free and intentional action. But we think that the concept of top down causation will provide the key. The short way of putting it is to say that the whole system, which is the whole person, has the top down influence on the neurobiological processes themselves. So there is a two-way interaction. Much of what goes into freedom, we think, has to do with one's past choices. Of course that sounds like an infinite regress, but it's not, because one is simply born active. To the extent that one is able to reprogram one's goals and values, to that extent one's actions become free. Warren makes a lot of use of the work of Antonio Damasio and the sort of development he has made in recognizing that if you examine a possible scenario for the future you decide [what is] good to enact or bad to enact. That has a causal impact on the likelihood of performing that action in the future. I wish I had the whole answer ready to lay out, but there's plenty of room for development there. Probably philosophers will say oh, you just came up with a new version of compatabilism, and I'm not sure I would object to that, because we have decided that no action is entirely free. That is there are always social and biological conditioning to our actions. If there were not, it would be such a random, irrational sort of thing that doesn't really count as what we are looking for.

Speaker 2: Two questions I guess. The first question refers to something I read in the research paper put out by the Templeton organization [*Research News and Opportunities in Science and Theology*]. The impression I had is verified by listening to your exquisite discussion, and I thank you. That has been very helpful. I am wondering if your entire research program is not really a question of the notion of the Christian tradition of mystery. Isn't this included somewhere, or how does that fit into your research program? But it seems to me that even Thomas Aquinas or all the way through the history of tradition the notion of mystery always exists. And when we talk about God, we are talking about mystery in the theological sense and, therefore, [I wonder] what is your purpose there. I'm not trying to be an anti-rationalist. But it seems that you are almost trying to reduce your research program to becoming God in the sense of the mind of God. Do you understand what I am saying?

Nancey Murphy: No, I don't. No I really don't. Sorry.

Speaker 2: The point I am getting at is that it seems to me that, in considering divine action in the world, there is always, for the Christian, a sense of mystery in God. We can't really know. What is your purpose? Do you see what I am getting at?

Nancey Murphy: Yes; now I do. Thanks. Referring to work that I've done on God's action in the world, I have written a paper on hypothesizing that if you want to talk scientifically about the point at which God acts in the world, you should pursue the quantum level. The reason for that is first the simple necessary conclusion that if God acts in, or on, all of God's creatures, then God necessarily acts at the quantum level. But also because there is the certain sort of indeterminacy there that allows you at evade talking about violations of laws of nature. But what I see myself doing there, and the rest of us who have been pursuing the problem of divine action for some years, is not really explaining what God is doing but trying to explain where in the world to look for God's action, presuming that it can be seen. That is, it's trying to solve an intellectual problem. How do you reconcile God's providential action with the supposition that God also acts by having predetermined laws of nature, etc.? Maybe that topic should just be thrown out because maybe it was simply a mistake to say that the laws of nature reflect God's will and it is irrational for God to violate them. I sometimes feel myself moving toward an interventionist position. But that is only to say that this is where in the world of science we should work if we want to talk about a way of reconciling our theological understanding of God's action with our scientific account of the world. But one of the things that Bob Russell and I have come to think, in the process of pursuing this issue is that God seems to have a preference of acting in ways that are never fully detectable by the objective observer. And so for instance if Polkinghorne is right and God acts in chaotic systems, well those are prime examples of cases where you would never know whether God was acting or not. Similarly, no one could ever know that God was acting at the quantum level either. As I think about what I know of divine action, one of the problems [that occurs to me] is if God does act in nature, why do we see so little of it? So there we are treading onto the edge of the problem of evil. But it seems to me that the sorts of things that Christians traditionally pray for are the sorts of things where one can never say with assurance that God did or did not answer their prayer. So we most often pray for people to get well, usually only if there is some hope that they will get well anyway. But that's lack of faith. Maybe that is the knowledge of the patterns of God's always acting in a hidden manner. So the mystery is still there, especially the question of why God does so little in the face of natural evil.

Speaker 3: In your remarks you said something that I took as rather negative about process theology. My question is going to be why you think that. Let me say a bit more of where I am coming from. Of course the exponents of process theology were Whitehead and Calvin Griffin. Calvin Griffin is a Californian, so you probably know him very well. Honestly as I read Whitehead I find his process very attractive, but I feel so sad that Whitehead died so early. He died at a ripe old age, but had he lived a little longer he would have understood some of the science a lot better than he did when he wrote some of these things. And when I read Calvin Griffin, I say that process can't be worth much because I really can't get much out of what he writes. But there are other thinkers more positive toward process [theology]. It happens that three of them I name are Catholic: Joe Bracken, Joseph Kazinski, and Jack Haught.

These people, I think, make a very compelling case that you can be a Christian, and that you can even be a Catholic in the face of higher Catholic hierarchy, who are usually opposed to process theology. Here are some rather courageous Catholic thinkers who like it anyway. Of course the classic reason why you should like processes is that it helps you out of the problem of evil and the theodicy problem. So my personal belief is that in the future, and the not so distant future, process theology in some form or other, probably not in the form of Calvin Griffin, is going to be extremely attractive. Now I want you to give me the counter case.

Nancey Murphy: Okay. I'm not completely sure where to start. One of my problems with process philosophy and process theology is the question, "what is the justification for this metaphysical system?" I am trained in analytic philosophy and I have some skepticism about one's ability to simply make up new concepts out of whole cloth. I think what the metaphysician does is examine the concepts that are already in use. They are justified by the fact that they are in use, because that shows that they work well. And so the metaphysician has the much more limited role of exploring our existing conceptual scheme, perhaps noting inconstancies or problems in trying to tune and fix it a little bit. But simply to create a new metaphysical system, I don't know how you can ever justify doing that.

Second, [there is a question] for the process theologians. If you have theological reasons for preferring, for instance, an understanding of God who is exemplified in the world God has created, then you have theological reasons for preferring that to your God. So why should you have to go out of the theological realm into metaphysics in order to bring back a metaphysical justification for something that you know theologically is a good move.

Third, my particular objection to the use of process theology, as I have seen it used by Ian Barbour and others, is, and I am not sure I have the word right, pan-psychism and pan-experientialism of Whitehead's thought. This is the view that if you have got consciousness at this high level of complexity, us, then in order to explain it there must be some very, very rudimentary form of consciousness in all of the lesser entities as well. And I think that is just a false explanatory move. The consciousness is explained by complexity of the system, not by its component parts already having consciousness of some rudimentary sort. This is somewhat a caricature, but it is almost like saying, "well, a human being is a very complex organism, so to explain that complexity all of its parts must have some rudimentary form of complexity." But that is obviously a fallacious argument.

Speaker 4: I understood you to say that to explain consciousness in a human being the consciousness must go all the way down to the least components of the human being. I don't think that's the way it is understood. If you say there is something in the dynamic activity at the lowest level that, at the highest level, becomes consciousness because of a complexity. This does not mean that atoms have consciousness in the sense that human beings have consciousness. There is a dynamic interaction in atoms, and anything lower than atoms, such that, at a higher and higher level, you get consciousness. But you are not trying to explain consciousness at the lowest levels, as I understand it.

Nancey Murphy: I was misrepresenting process thought to some extent. I am thinking particularly of Whitehead and the fact that experience is one of his basic metaphysical categories. And I have never heard a process thinker explain to my satisfaction why that should be called experience. But Ian Barbour does argue explicitly that process thought explains consciousness in that it postulates something rudimentary and analogous to it at the simplest level.

Speaker 5: I would like to come back to the issue of God's actions, which you discussed last night. Particularly I want to consider your comments last night as well as your comments this morning that we look for it at the quantum level or at the chaotic system level. So there are two parts. One is the question: "Isn't that kind of a nice theoretical

God of the gaps move?" We have a nice theoretical base now. We think we are never going to be able to fill that gap, so it's going to be safe for a long time. Second, [can you] tie this back into your comments last night about reviving the physicalism and the Hebraic understanding of the body as the soul, as the whole person, in particularly the resurrection of the body? Is the resurrection of the body the result of a chaotic system or quantum event, or if it is a new body as you described last night, why is the empty tomb such an important part? What happened to the old body? And would you talk more about resurrection as it fits into physicalism and the way in which God acts in the world?

Nancey Murphy: First, the God of the gaps issue. If it turns out that scientists can explain quantum behavior deterministically then we are simply back where we were before, with the understanding of the natural processes as determined by natural laws, or at least describable by natural laws. We will then be forced to choose whether God works through those natural processes or God intervenes at some point. I would be unhappy if that aspect of my thinking turns out not to have the advantages that it does. But it is no great catastrophe. Regarding resurrection, a lot of people think of Jesus' resurrection as a miracle in the same sort of sense as say Jesus' raising of Lazarus. But I would follow Pannenberg and others who say this is actually an eschatological event happening out of its place in history. We simply can't talk in physics terms about that, because the current eon is governed by the laws of physics as we know them. The only thing we know about the next eon is that it is not. So just as we can't think back before the big bang, we can't think ahead of the end of this universe in its current physical form. So I think it is not only impossible, but it is inappropriate to try and talk in scientific terms about what happened in the resurrection.

Now regarding the empty tomb, if my colleague is right who suggests that we think of each of us as being resurrected at the moment of death, then we have an anomaly that Jesus' body was obviously either transformed or, poof, gone, something like that. You can handle that by saying well, it is what God did in order to make us understand that it was transformation rather than a ghost or whatever. But it would be much neater in a sense if our resurrections all followed the same pattern. If whatever is left of our bodies, that is all of the atoms left in our graves or urns, is actually transformed at the resurrection, then there is a happy continuity between this life and the next. Whether it has anything more than symbolic nature, I am not sure, because what makes me me, is not the material I am made out of, but it is my personality, my interpersonal relationships, etc. I would prefer it if when we are resurrected that we do actually appear where our graves were and all that sort of thing.

Speaker 5: Let me see if I understand you. You're saying that the resurrection is a singularity of the eschatological world that touches this world as a medium. It is a one time only event.

Nancey Murphy: Yes.

Speaker 5: There is nothing you can lay it on directly, because it's a singularity.

Nancey Murphy: Oh, No! It's the only clue from God as to the fate of ourselves and the rest of the universe. So we can't say anything about it in terms of its natural causes or what is happening in physics terms. It is absolutely crucial in talking about the rest of the human race and the cosmos as a whole is looking forward to. One of the important things about the resurrection story is that the texts portray Jesus, after the resurrection, in such a wide variety of ways. For example, these vary from Paul's vision, which some religions would call a body of light, to the much more concrete appearances where he can fish and all that sort of thing. So the text is saying what we can't say: what a resurrected person is really like. At the one end it is a whole lot different from these physical solid bodies that we have got now, but at the other end it is still recognizably continuous the person you were before.

Speaker 5: It is also an exception to the way God works in the world.

Nancey Murphy: Right! As Pannenberg would say, it's a violation of the laws of nature now, but it's a foretaste of the laws of nature as they will be in the next beyond.

Speaker 6: I would like to speak to the comment that in process theology we are introducing a new metaphysics for no good reason. I think there are several reasons that are coming to us out of science that make this something we have to take into account. Just to sum them up, one of them is that many scientific thinkers today are thinking that the dynamics of things are at least as basic as the stuff they are made from. Even going to the lowest level of physics, energy and matter are more or less the same. We can't just say the stuff that is sitting there is basic. If energy is involved, then these things are always in process anyway. You have a concept of the universe as dynamic rather than static. I think that has to be taken into account when you are doing metaphysics. You can't have static metaphysics and take this into account. This is seen as the process of emergence. If things are self-organizing, and when you go to different levels, you have a different sort of thing happening, an emergence, and you have, as an example, consciousness. And you are talking about a top-down motivation [causality] then you have to take into account again that this is dynamic and the interaction between levels, at least as far as we see in nature, runs both ways. You can then, in fact, make the argument that processes [theology] is at least as basic. For example, you could argue that maybe the brain is stuff, but the mind is the process that is involved with that stuff that makes up the brain. Perhaps if you think our identity is more our mind than our brain, you could say the processes are more vital in who we are than the statusness of who we are. This stems from the information theory. So I think this has to be introduced, even though it is coming to us from left field, from the scientific thinking of our age.

Nancey Murphy: I can halfway assent to everything you said, but then ask the question where you add to that by making everybody read *Process and Reality*. You just gave a much better account of nature in the world that I know than Whitehead does and was entirely intelligible to everyone in this room.

Speaker 6: I don't think you have to make everybody read *Process and Reality*.

Nancey Murphy: Well, what is different about having a process metaphysic than your understanding of the world as very dynamic in the process?

Speaker 6: I don't think there is a lot of difference. I don't think we necessarily have to think of Whitehead as defining the field. I think the speakers that were quoted went far beyond Whitehead.

Nancey Murphy: My question is what do you gain beyond our knowledge about the extent to which the world is a matter of process, by doing metaphysics? So this goes back to my first answer to John's question. I simply question that there is a discipline that gives us knowledge about the world that somehow goes beyond, or is independent, of what we know about the world through all our disciplines.

Speaker 6: Except that people are going to begin to think metaphysically, once they get this in their heads as something we must take into account. It will affect our metaphysical suppositions if we start to take some of these other thoughts seriously.

Nancey Murphy: Maybe we are using metaphysics in a different sense. I am talking about it as a distinct philosophical enterprise, as Whitehead and others have done. I see no point in doing that. I see no justification for it. If you talk about metaphysics simply in terms of our having categories and terms, and intend to apply rather generally to the things we know in the world, I would just call that talking, not doing metaphysics.

Speaker 6: Okay.

Speaker 7: Nancey, last night you mentioned the twin problems of binding and consciousness from the neuroscientific perspective. Damasio and some others are doing some work around that. I began thinking of the whole notion of self as a construct as well, which I would understand as a more inclusive concept than soul. But I am interested in your understanding of the relationship. I am particularly wondering if the construct of self as an extension of consciousness is another concept that will undergo change.

Nancey Murphy: I haven't read Damasio's more recent book, so he would probably be a lot of help there. I just joined a group of Christian scholars who are planning to get together once a month for intellectual discussion. One of the topics that was proposed as our first subject was "the self." I thought, "I don't know what that term means." I certainly know how to use "self" reflexively and talk about myself, but I think that's just a grammatical trick. I know also that in the psychology field there are lots of theories about what the self is as distinguished from evil, etc. But I don't even know that there is any uniform usage of the term. If the term is going to be used I think it is going to have to be introduced with a stipulative definition. Maybe that is just a terminological response. The more interesting question is how do we come to have what is often known as the sense of self. Is that closer to what you are talking about? I am by no means up on the literature here, but my impression is that having a sense of self is actually a very complex neurobiological achievement. We know this primarily because of abnormal cases where people don't have that sense. So for instance, there are people who will complain to their doctors that someone else has taken over their husband's body, so his self is no longer his self. I think there are also cases where people feel that they are aliens of their own bodies. So they have lost this sense of "this is I, I am this." So for those who object, on dualist grounds, that you have to have a soul, in order to have a sense of self, I think the empirical evidence is going to begin stacking up to the contrary. Rather, the sense of self comes later in development.

Child psychologists can probably tell us when this begins to develop. So it seems to be not the basis of consciousness, as someone like Kant would have said, but actually it is at the high end of development of conscious processes.

Speaker 8: It occurs to me that most of our questions on these matters, and perhaps it must be that way, are from the point of view of what has happened since the New Testament times and the Church. That is, we are interpreting the New Testament faith rather than what preceded the New Testament faith. And then in turn we interpret the New Testament faith in terms of what preceded. For example, Klaus Westerman pointed out to me years ago, not to me personally, but through his writing, that we are mistaken about the idea that God is always intervening. We are mistaken because God *is* intervening. For example, Adam sins and Eve sins and God is there, and Cain sins and God is there, and the whole human race sins and God is there, so it looks like everything is intervention. And in the resurrection there is intervention. But he points out that the fact is that there is also blessing. And God blessed! And that blessing is, in a sense, intervention if you want to call it that, although it is not intervention in the usual sense. It's that God empowers Adam and Eve and God empowers the human race in the blessing from one generation to another as you have it when Abraham blesses Isaac, and Isaac blesses Jacob, and so on. Jacob blesses Joseph in that way. So that not only do we need to correct the science of the 17th century, but we also need to correct our present theology in terms of the biblical faith, and say, "hey, our theology has been wrong." As Westerman has pointed out, yeah it is intervention, but everything is intervention and also a blessing. It is empowerment for nature and for reproductive possibilities, etc.

Nancey Murphy: I think that's helpful. I guess I want something as a matter of clarification. My tendency, and that of those with whom I work on the divine action problem, is to say that divine intervention has almost a technical sense of God's violating the laws of nature. That means, of course, that to talk about it in terms of the Hebrew Bible is anachronistic, because [then] we didn't have the modern conception of the laws of nature. What I would like to talk about is special divine actions, rather than miracles and interventions. That is, if Sarah achieves the ability to conceive at a late age it would seem to be as much affecting her biology in a positive way as, say, intervening as some sort of punishment. I think it is good to keep in mind that the acts we are trying to explain are usually acts of blessing, but it doesn't really help with the modern problem of divine action.

Speaker 8: I would feel that, in a Biblical sense, intervention should be interpreted as turning history around. For example, Israel is in slavery. Okay, they're going to stay there. No, because God turns history around. And that whatever it is logically or naturally, does not make a whole lot of difference as far as the Bible is concerned I don't think. The main point is that the community has experienced a turn around that they didn't expect.

Nancey Murphy: Yes, I think that is a good point. If you get too busy worrying about where in science you can talk about divine action, you don't want to lose the big picture, which is the pattern of what God does with that ability to act.

Speaker 8: So the main thing about resurrection is not the physics of how it happened, but the experience of what happened. Instead of going fishing, Peter does something else that he never expected to be doing.

Chair: Nancey, do you want to respond to what Speaker 8 has said?

Nancey Murphy: No. I think this is fine.

Chair: Speaker 8, were you expecting a response?

Speaker 8: Are you giving me another chance to talk? (laughter)

Chair: No. (laughter) I have the next question from Speaker 9.

Speaker 9: Haught was mentioned. His new book, *God after Darwin*, I think really deals with an evolutionary theology and science that goes beyond Whitehead and the world of process [theology]. I just want to tell you a little story about Einstein and Niels Bohr. Einstein was very troubled about the uncertainty principle and he said to Niels Bohr, "God doesn't play dice." And you never hear what Niels Bohr said back to Einstein. He said, "Albert, don't tell God what to do." Now I think there is a lot to what he said: "Don't tell God what to do." And that's the theme of John Haught's new book. He's from Georgetown. In his new book he asks if God does offer a world of both law and chance, and there is the dice part, and this is how God acts in the world of process, why does God do this? Because God wants to be sure the world knows it's other than God! Get away from pantheism! The world is something other than God. And so God allows the world to play dice – a world of law and chance. We know that in chaotic systems, which are chance, there is really self-organization. So it's the intellithy of the world, the essence of the world, to play at both law and chance. And that's how God's action takes place in the world. It's the intellithy of an acorn to become an oak. It's the intellithy of the world to be a world of law and chance. Now that is how process theology has gone way beyond Whitehead, and Hartshorne, and Cobb, and Griffin. We are still thinking about God's action. Now what do you think of his idea?

Nancey Murphy: I haven't read that book yet.

Speaker 9: Read it. It's tremendous!

Speaker 10: I wanted to follow on this idea of Haught and *God after Darwin* and the universe of both law and chance. I think, perhaps, even if you haven't read the book yet, you may still be able to comment on this concept. As I understand it, God creates a universe that is not just an appendage of himself. He gives that universe some degree of autonomy because otherwise it would merely be an appendage. And then he gives this universe a degree of latitude, or elbow-room, or freedom through chance processes. Consequently, the universe has the opportunity to explore possibilities, especially evolutionary possibilities. It is not hard-wired. God doesn't push buttons, and pull strings. Sometimes, when I have to explain this to undergraduates and to my non-academic friends, I say this is kind of extending the free will idea to the rest of the universe, not just humans. They usually respond by asking, "well, what does that do to God's sovereignty though?" This is sort of the question in my mind as well. The other question is, "is it even fair to draw that analogy?" Can you talk about giving the universe freedom through chance and contingency, and nondeterministic processes? Because the inanimate universe doesn't have a mind. So are we conflating an analogy with reality here? So that's one problem that I have with this more advanced form of process philosophy. Then there is the old problem: how do you reconcile that with God's sovereignty? Where do you find the balance? In our department at Anderson we are discussing chapter by chapter Haught's previous book, *Science and Religion from Conflict to Conversation*, that foreshadows some of these notions. Do you have any thoughts at all on this matter?

Nancey Murphy: Well, only to agree with you entirely. It seems entirely true that the universe changes and develops by use of a combination of law and chance. You can even use computer programs to show that the best way to reach a solution to a novel problem is to randomly generate possible solutions and then have some selective mechanism. What you say about the relationship between chance processes and free will is exactly right. It's an analogy. As long as you remember it is an analogy, not an identity, you are perfectly fine. In fact I have used that analogy myself and I think there is something in my paper for later this morning on that subject, but I can't remember for sure.

Speaker 5: To play on this role of rule and chance, an illustration or an analogy that I heard once that is helpful, is that when humans create worlds we do it in the same way. When we create games like football, we create a definite field and we mark it off in ten yard marks. We have four downs, or whatever you want. We have sixty minutes [total play-time]. We have very clear rules. We would have a very boring game if it weren't for the fact that the players in the game have a lot of freedom. They can move here and they can move there. They can run. They can pass. They can kick. So we create worlds with definite rules and a system. But we also create a lot of freedom inside them. And that is what makes an interesting world. So as by analogy, perhaps that is the kind of world God has created.

Nancey Murphy: Umhmm [yes].

Speaker 4: I'm wondering why we don't take the vast unknown relation in terms of the highest field, through the experience of man and of God coming into his life. A very good example is the experience of St. John of the Cross. He was asked the question, "How do you know you have experienced God?" He said, "Because when I least want him, somehow he is there. When I most want him, somehow he is not there." So this is not a creation of my imagination. In the resurrection experience there are also examples of this sort. It is not an example of recognizing Christ, it is always an example of Christ's revealing himself by what he does and by what he says. Especially there is the example of the Lukan account of the people on the way to Emmaus. They spend two or three hours talking with him. Only at the moment he chooses is there self-revelation. Only when he chooses to say, "Give me something to eat," are they sure he is not a ghost. Also when he said to cast the net on the other side of the boat, they were not expecting it at all. It was the last thing in the world they expected. It is one thing to try to understand on one level, but it's another to consider the experience itself. So why not speak about God's coming into life? It's one thing to try to understand it at some level. But it's another thing to look at the experience itself. It's really what the whole scripture is about. It's about our (man's) experience with God from beginning to end. If we want to think about it in philosophical terms, fine. I think we need to do that. But that doesn't explain it. It helps, but it doesn't really explain it. It helps us to understand a bit. Our limited ability to understand is not at the level of God's.

Speaker 11: Maybe it's a tired old expression that text without context is pretext. When you were speaking yesterday about the Hebraic conception of resurrection, my question is which Hebraic conception? There isn't a single Hebraic conception. There is an evolution of a conception in the Old Testament, as I understand it. And then there is the context in which Jesus addresses the issue, which is also informed by discussions that were going on in Pharisaic Judaism at the time, which was a highly Helenized Judaism. Many scholars are pointing out that there is no pure Hebraic thought at the time of Jesus. This was a Hellenistic society, in which a lot of the uses of the concept of the survival of the soul in an intermediate state were actually being debated. So my question is how is your own thinking different from [that of a] neoplatonist who reads back what he wants to read in the New Testament? It seems like it's the negative complement of the God of the gaps. It's sort of the subordination of theology to scientific theory. Could you comment on that?

Nancey Murphy: I guess I don't really understand your question. I'm happy to have you point out that there was no single concept of resurrection. I don't think I ever talked about *the Hebrew* concept of resurrection. I talked about a development in Hebrew thought where the question of resurrection was raised sometime before Jesus' day.

Speaker 11: What I am asking is: are you deciding, by reading something into the text, what Jesus meant? You suggested yesterday in your lecture that in some sense you were getting back to the original intent of the scripture by proposing this model. I am asking how is this different from anyone else who looks for another theme, which could as easily have been a context for what Jesus was saying?

Nancey Murphy: There are two questions there. One is, "Am I on solid ground in saying that getting back to a concept of resurrection of body, instead of immortality of the soul, is getting back to original Christian teaching?" I don't think there is any question about that.

[Then] I haven't said that the Bible teaches physicalism. I have said the New Testament does not clearly teach dualism. So my position is that scripture is actually indefinite on that and in fact I said these were not questions that the Biblical writers tended to raise or wanted to answer.

Speaker 3: I would like to make a brief comment on what was just said regarding the various concepts of resurrection in the bible. I just heard a very wonderful presentation this past Wednesday evening. There is a New Testament scholar at the Lutheran School of Theology named Barbara Rossi who, for various reasons, was speaking about the Old Testament, which is not her academic specialty. She was specifically asked to do a study on the passage of the dry bones in Ezekiel. She talked at some length about the thread in the Old Testament of a communal resurrection. It isn't the resurrection of the individual body necessarily that Ezekiel is talking about but rather the resurrection of the entire house of Israel. That's the way the rhetoric goes in Ezekiel. So there is an additional component to the discussion.

Speaker 12: Would you comment on your (this is directed to Nancey) distinction between self and identity. Does that add anything? Are they the same? Or how do you interpret that? I've heard identity used in a variety of ways.

Nancey Murphy: Well, I don't use the term *self* as a technical term. But in response to John, I was talking about one's sense of self, which is an aspect of our consciousness. I would see that as clearly related to, and perhaps synonymous with, a sense of personal identity. But I do not have any distinct technical ways of using those terms. I simply use them as the English language does.

Speaker 8: I would like to comment on what Speaker 3 has said. And I am in awe of myself that I would dare to do that. (laughter) I would like to point out that [what he said] is exactly right. What appears in Ezekiel was a communal resurrection, and was not a resurrection in terms of being resurrected, as we would understand the concept, from the dead. For Israel, it was a spiritual and political resurrection in the sense that they were going back to where they had come from, out of the exile. But they were not just going back. They were resurrected to an entirely different plane of life there in the new Palestine. This was a plane with a new heart and a new mind. And it is going to be out of that rather than the external law which gives them obedience and a new life. There is a communal resurrection. But the communal resurrection is defined differently. And I think in a way this may be helpful in terms of Paul's understanding of what the resurrection is for us today. It is a new quality of life. And so these are not antithetical concepts at all. They are very close together. But then when you come to the New Testament that is also, contrary to most popular understanding, a communal concept. Even in one of the Gospels it talks about people walking around, who were dead, in the streets of Jerusalem. That makes it a little more difficult to believe in the resurrection. But there is the concept of what Paul is saying: Jesus is the first fruits of those who were dead and the rest is going on.

Speaker 3: I'm glad that you said that resurrection in Ezekiel is spiritual, because it says that explicitly in the Ezekiel text: Yaweh says to Ezekiel, "prophesy to the spirit." That is, to *Ruach*, the Spirit meaning breath, and breathe spirit, breath, and life into these bones. That's what the Old Testament very clearly says.

Speaker 8: And that very passage has *Ruach, Ruach, Ruach* in it about three or four different ways. One being the spirit of God, one being the spirit of man, and the other just being like you said, the wind. So how are you going to translate this stuff?

II.
Saturday Afternoon

Saturday Afternoon Session 1. This immediately follows lunch. Under discussion are both public lectures and all of the previous discussion.

Speaker 13: I want to sort of re-traverse the territory you covered this morning trying to give us an alternative creation ethic to the natural law tradition that we all know and some love and some loathe. You also want to tie this into your account of how God acts in the world. It seems that you take it down to the micro level and the quantum level, and there you find indeterminacy and so forth, and places where God can sort of slip into the world, non-coercively. And then the picture becomes the basis of a natural law and non-violent ethic. Then this is going to cohere with your understanding of your reading of evolutionary theory with God siding with the prey, not the predator. And then of course, connecting this up with God's being revealed most perfectly at the cross (or whatever). Here is the question. At the ethical level, the level of Christian ethics, there is of course pluralism in the tradition, and that is what we are dealing with. At the level of reading evolutionary theory, there again is plural underdetermination. There is more than one way to side with the predator or with the prey, and whether you do may well reflect value choices or commitments simply outside of sciences. Darwin read malfeasance into nature. But at the quantum level, and here is the clincher, what we find is a world that isn't fully determined and there is a non-coercive moment when electrons transition from one atomic state to another and so forth.

But here too there is pluralism. There are of course fully deterministic alternatives to the standard indeterministic quantum theory. So at that level you have a choice to make as well. And it seems that what the overall argument is is that you've got coherence between a non-violent ethic, and a nature in evolution, but at the same time in the process of redemption. Where the prey is is where we find God, and then the indeterminism at the micro level. But you can also have coherence. Now I don't know that deterministic quantum mechanics presages Constantinian Christianity, and Malthusian economics and whether survival of the fitness is right there in deterministic quantum theory. But at any rate you have choices at each level that brings you a coherent overall picture. And I am sympathetic with that. But where is the fulcrum here? Do you fix the cross? Do you say my most basic commitment, a focus on the cross and suffering and so forth and then work your way down, or is the best evidence of indeterminism in quantum theory in working your way up, or is it somewhere in the middle. Where is the fulcrum of all this?

Nancey Murphy: I don't think you need a fulcrum until someone can come along and make the alternative consistent system. That is why I am saying come on, do it, show me. The paper that I gave today was an attempt to set out, in forty-five minutes length, the kind of argument that George Ellis and I made in our book *On the Moral Nature of the Universe*. One of the hardest things we had to do in writing that book together was to decide on the direction in which to run the argument. George wanted to start with science and argue to theology and I said no, you can't do that. You aren't going to get a strong enough argument. He said that if you start with theology you lose everybody who doesn't already agree with the theology. So what we ended up doing was a sort of dialectical argument and ended with the claim that it's actually the coherence of the system that makes the argument. We do talk considerably about both Imre Lakatos' and Allister MacIntyre's accounts of how you adjudicate between competing scientific theories or rival traditions and have done some work in that direction. But of course, not in this space of forty-five minutes. The real point to make in answering your question, though, is the argument for divine action at the quantum level is not really based on indeterminacy. The argument for divine action at the quantum level is based on theologically unexceptional claims. God is immanent in the whole of creation, and so I would take exception to talking about God slipping in in the indeterminacies. I think that is perhaps where my account of divine action at the quantum level differs from Pollard's, although it has been much too long since I read his book. So I am claiming that all of us think of God as immanent within, and acting within, the whole of creation. The question then is: just what does that amount to in terms of divine direction of the process. Is it, as I was saying, a rubber stamp, or is it occasionalism? We hope neither. The reason for emphasizing God's action at the quantum level is not simply the truism that God must be acting there, but the advantage it gives you. If in fact some of the processes are indeterministic, [you still make the claim] that God is not violating God's own laws. If determinism turns out to be true at the quantum level that doesn't defeat the claim that God is acting at that level. It just means that you are back to the age old, three hundred year-old, program of how to reconcile divine action with natural processes.

Speaker 13: You said that there was no need for a fulcrum as long as there was no alternative. Are you saying that you couldn't construct a coherent system here with a natural law ethic as traditionally construed and a nature red and tooth and claw that would cohere?

Nancey Murphy: I don't know. But so long as nobody else produces one, you don't have any way to settle the difference between yourself and your rival. So I understand rationality as comparative, rather than absolute, justification of any particular point of view. It [the alternate system] needs to be on the table, and then you make a further step of saying why this system, more or less as coherent as that one, is better. I will resort to something like Lakatos' notion of progress, or McIntyre's claim that sometimes you can show the superiority of one tradition over its rival by being able to show that yours can explain the rival's failures, whereas the rival can't explain them that well.

Speaker 8: I went along with something this morning that I don't feel comfortable with at all, and that is that the fall is not historical. The fall is very historical. But we need to realize that the fall is a description of the present creation. And what is not historical then is the creation story in the Bible. That is the eschatological reading. Okay? Do you go along with that?

Nancey Murphy: I think that creation, fall, redemption, and final transformation are not rigidly separable stages in God's action, but could more readily be seen as themes interpenetrating throughout cosmic history.

Speaker 8: The only other Eden story in the Bible is in Ezekiel. I can't think of the chapter right now. But the point is that for Ezekiel the fall is the fall of the king of Tyre. I spent a lot of time thinking about that over the years. I think that may be a very significant point that Ezekiel was making there. Then the fall puts the emphasis on power and social organization and social structure. It is a little bit like Job's criticism of God. Now [consider] Job in the prose section, after he passes the test, regarding whether he had good motives or not. In fact he passes two tests. How did he pass them? He said, "The Lord gives and the Lord takes away, blessed be the name of the Lord." It's okay. And so he blesses the Lord. The only thing is that in the poetic section he calls God a cosmic bully. The whole problem with the universe is not a case of the justice of God, but it's a question of power. That's where the point is. And God is just a cosmic power bolt. The whole book of Job is ambiguous as far as its answer goes to the problem of evil. It's a wisdom book. And that's about as far as wisdom can go. Wisdom is based on the creation of this world, more or less. I think you have to go to the prophetic to get answers beyond the book of Job, which would be Exodus, which has the concept of promise and redemption; and then the book of Second Isaiah, which looks at the servant motif.

So what I am saying is that the wisdom of the Bible anticipated your answers.

Nancey Murphy: (laughter) It's always good to hear that there's evidence for the truth of the Scriptures.

Speaker 14: In the historical reading of story of Adam and Eve, you've come across the lines that there was no sickness, death, and so forth, and the biological record doesn't seem to support that very well. I'm wondering if there isn't some way to reach some kind of unity here. The only reason I bring this up is maybe by analogy with the working cosmology by this fellow Schroeder over in Israel who talks about creation being both six-days and fifteen billion years. The point is that it depends on looking at it from different viewpoints. If you were to have a collection of early humans or pre hominids or something like that who, perhaps for lack of memory, lack of intelligence or something like that, did not know they were going to die, did not know about sickness, did not know any of these things, would it be reasonable to say that in that life they did not experience sickness, ignorance, death, etc.? Therefore, although life in this Eden-like condition was not all that great, they did not have the knowledge or experience of the bad things until they had advanced to a level. That is until they had advanced to such a level that they were able to interact with God in the way represented metaphorically in the story of Adam and Eve in Eden.

Nancey Murphy: Well, animals apparently are not aware of the fact of their own death, so one can imagine hominids also not being aware of that. But I can't see how you can imagine them not being aware of sickness and not being aware of death in general. So that seems a fairly incredible notion to me. But more importantly, I am not sympathetic to the apparent need to reconcile speculations about hominid past with particular details of the story because I don't see the story as intended to be a historical account.

Speaker 8: What story is this?

Nancey Murphy: The first two chapters of Genesis

Speaker 8: Well, I would say I don't know of any reputable interpreter of the Bible who holds that the seven days of creation are to be taken literally. Usually the statement is made is that is a systematic device.

How could you remember it? Well, the seven days of the week. They have it all down pat, as in a child's mind. I think we ought to have our children learn it, so they can have something to fight against the rest of their lives. (laughter)

Nancey Murphy: Then if the requirements had only been five, then God would have rested for the weekend. (laughter)

Speaker 15: Is the sequence correct in Genesis 1 and 2?

Speaker 3: No it's not correct, Gene. It's almost correct. But then you need to make three transpositions and then it will be correct.

Nancey Murphy: Oh, tell us.

Speaker 3: Oh, I don't have a Bible in front of me and I don't remember which three they are. If Carl can pass me a Bible, well … (laughter)

Speaker 8: (In the background) Okay, let's let him point out what those things are. But this is intolerable.

Speaker 3: God had the earth bring forth vegetation, plants and the seed and so on and God said, "Let there be lights in the dome of the sky to separate the day from the night." Well, you've got to put that before the vegetation. You've got to have day and night coming earlier than verse 14. So there is something you've got to do. And, "Let the waters bring forth swarms of living creatures. Let birds fly above the earth." Then later on there are the creatures that creep on the ground. The reptiles in Genesis come later than birds. You've got to do a transposition there. You get the point? It's not bad. I look at this as a very poetic evolutionary document, which has a few scientific transpositions to make and then you have to re-interpret the Hebrew word *Yom* and then you've got it.

Speaker 9: Yes and also in the first chapter men and women are made together, and in the second chapter women came from the rib of Adam. So there is a very different story there.

Chair: Speaker 8 has said that this is intolerable. So I think we are going to get a ...

Speaker 8: I would ordinarily not speak out for a third time, but from the biblical point of view, you say it is incorrect. From the biblical point of view the biblical statement is very good! And from biblical perspective, that is from the writer's perspective, it's correct! Now from our scientific perspective, from the scientific point of view, you say that it's incorrect. When we say that we are judging his perspective by our perspective. What you've got to do is go back to his perspective and look at it in the light of other perspectives from other cultures of his time. How can we say that his perspective is wrong and ours is right? Well because we judge his by ours. If he were doing the judging, which of course he couldn't do, he would say that his is correct and ours is wrong, because he isn't looking at it from the way we look at it.

Nancey Murphy: Well, I think the more important point to make is that for all the fun we can have working on these harmonizations, I would never dream of doing that in my class because it would just encourage a large number of my students to think that is the way you ought to read those stories. So it's not that there are two accounts and one of them is accurate by one person's lights, and the other is accurate by someone else's. The point is that they are not intended to do the same thing at all.

Speaker 8: Exactly. You should not ask whether the Bible is literal. It is to be interpreted by the *intention* of the writer. That makes quite a difference. If you have to argue, this was not the intention.

Speaker 10: I was debating in my mind whether or not to go into this, but I choose not to. (laughter) There was a previous comment that puzzled me: the idea that God sides with the prey, because at some level everything is prey. Almost everything has a predator. Then when we get to the top predators like the great white sharks, and killer whales, and lions, they all have parasites. So at some level everything is prey. So I am puzzled by the statement that God sides with the prey, because at some level everything is prey.

Nancey Murphy: Well that is not intended to mean that God picks out some creatures that God favors over the others. It's intended as a comment on which role in the animal kingdom sheds more light on the nature of reality when you think the nature of reality is God governed, God determined. So in so far you are being preyed upon and not killing in return, then you're playing that role. But insofar as you're preying upon someone else, you're not.

Speaker 2: I had a teacher in theology, John Courtney Murray, I was just getting back to the biblical scholar's [Speaker 8's] question. This is very interesting for us, or for me anyway. He claimed that, in the interpretation of the Exodus story of the burning bush, there were three strata of understanding. So you really have to be careful. The Bible that I use says, "I am Who I Am," or "I am to be," or "Who are you?" when Moses asked the question. And he claimed that was a Greek interpretation in more of the Septuagenarian tradition. But then he (Murray) said, in his opinion, now he was a theologian, not a scripture scholar, but in his opinion, the second strata was a kind of intercultural thing deeply imbedded in the root of his understanding of "I am the cause." That is there is a causal inference here: "I am the cause." And then he (Murray) said: "However, that's not what Moses heard." Or as at the author's time, this is not the original Hebrew interpretation of what's written down. "I shall be there as who I am, shall I be there." That's the way he wrote it: "I shall be there, as who I am shall I be there." Now that's his interpretation of that text. It's really interesting, now you have to go back to understand it. Of course you have to go back and ask, "what does that really mean?" Of course he was a theologian and not a scripture scholar.

Speaker 15: But the Hebrew doesn't have the present tense. He means: "I will be that I will be."

Speaker 2: Well, the way he wrote it is: "I shall be there. I am. I am." And of course Etienne Gilson, the French philosopher, picked that up in trying to defend the Thomistic interpretation of God whose essence was to exist. God's essence is to exist for a philosopher like that. What would you say about that?

Speaker 8: Well, I would point out that we have a linguist here with a doctorate from Harvard. I don't know why he doesn't speak up.

Speaker 16: I wouldn't venture to say that the way it was heard in that original context is the way we read it. It is true that there is no present tense, but the verb is in non-perfective, so that it is either future or durative in the present. I like the idea, in fact that formula *'ehyeh 'asher 'ehyeh*, is mirrored a little bit later where the second *'ehyeh* is replaced by *yhwh*. So it is usually interpreted as Yahweh, the name of the God of Israel, as a causative of the verb to be, and that is probably where the notion of causation came in. I find that very nice. You can get that from the language, But you can also get "I am who I am" or "I am that I am," it's all possible. It depends a bit on what goal you are trying to reach in interpretation.

Speaker 1: This morning, in the response to an entirely different question, you said something to the effect that God acts only in such a way that the action cannot be observed by an objective observer.

Nancey Murphy: I said that you can't be sure that God had acted.

Speaker 1: Okay. I was a little puzzled by that particularly in light of the talk that you gave subsequently. If we accept that premise does that reveal something about God?

Nancey Murphy: Well, John Pick has the thesis that God's existence needs to be ambiguous or veiled in order to leave us free to respond or not. I keep trying to figure out whether I think that's true or not. It certainly is true that I have no choice in believing whether this microphone is here or not. If you see it you can't help but believe it's there. If God's revelation is much more obvious and unambiguous doesn't that require you to believe that God exists? If that's the case, does it detract from human freedom in responding to God? I'm not sure. When George Ellis and I were writing together, he was very much taken by that argument. He argued that one of the reasons that we see evidence of God's providence as so ambiguous is so that people don't obey God simply because God rewards those who obey God and causes misfortune to fall on those who don't. So I haven't made up my mind about that. But it just seems empirically true to me of the cases we know of, when we attribute an event to a special act of God, that someone could always contest it. And it seems to me that we tend to pray habitually for things (That is there are certain things we pray for and certain things we don't.) for which we will never know for sure that the result was divine action. So one of the reasons that people say if God already knows what we need then why do we have to pray? If what I'm saying is true then one of the reasons for prayer is that it provides one of the markers to know that this was a divine act rather than simply coincidence.

Nancey Murphy, at this time observed the group was not bubbling over with questions and indicated that she would be happy for anyone's comments, without their being in the form of a question.

Chair: That is appropriate. We also do not need to deal only with the last lecture. One of the students commented to me that it would be interesting to deal more with the neurosciences again.

Speaker 10: Can you elaborate more on the idea that prayer is a marker? I have often heard the comment that if God already knows what is going to happen, then prayer doesn't change God, it changes us. Or prayer just means that you align yourself with God's will. But I had never heard it described as a marker. Could you elaborate on that?

Nancey Murphy: What I mean by that is that it is part of the narrative that allows us to pick out certain events as divine actions. Here is a case in point: In my Charismatic days, a woman in my group asked us to pray one evening that she would conceive a baby. She and her husband had been trying for about eight years. She did get pregnant, and counting backwards from when she knew she was pregnant, it was very likely that she got pregnant on that very night. Well, if we hadn't prayed, Oxana still would have been pregnant. Would we have attributed that in any special way to God's action? Or would we simply have said "Ah, finally!"

Speaker 15: (background) So, do prayers count or not?

Speaker 10: How does that make it a marker? How does prayer relate to the event?

Nancey Murphy: Give up on the word marker. What I mean is the fact that we pray is part of the narrative context that allows us to recognize some of these ambiguous events, events that could have been mere coincidence, as God's acts because they come at a time that makes them appear responsive to our requests.

Speaker 10: So if I understand you correctly, it could very well be that God intended her to get pregnant at a particular time. But the fact that you prayed about it makes you a little more aware of God's activity. Is that what you are saying?

Nancey Murphy: Yes. And also I think we often pray for things because we think God prompts us to. Why did she choose that particular night to ask us to pray that she would conceive? Why didn't she ask us two months before? So sometimes I think we can find out what God intends to do by noticing what we find ourselves praying for.

Speaker 15: But that is determinism. We are, therefore, not free: we are *determined*. I don't believe that!

Nancey Murphy: I don't believe it either. I think it's a faulty argument. When the problem was raised, which was centuries ago, the term for knowledge was *scientia*, and scientia meant knowledge about that which was determinate. If that is how you define knowledge, and you say that God knows, then you do, in fact, have a logical problem to sort out as to how something can be contingent but also known. But we do not define knowledge, any of the sorts of knowledge except logical truths, in that way. And we are not bothered by the fact that God knows the truths of logic. So it's necessarily the case if God knows something that it's going to happen. But the order of dependence is the other way around. God knows it's going to happen because it's going to happen. It's not that it's going to happen because God knows it. So if you're freely going to decide to wash your car tomorrow then God knows that today, and God's knowing of it today is brought about by the fact that you wash the car tomorrow. Your washing the car tomorrow is not brought about by God's knowing it.

Speaker 15: What about the alternate choice of the human? Does God know each of the alternate choices according to the person who makes the choice?

Nancey Murphy: What do you mean by alternate choice?

Speaker 15: The choice between God or no God, heaven or hell.

Nancy Murphy: As result, yes. But I do not see that as determining the choice.

Speaker 15: To me that is a contradiction. I am sorry. If God knows then it's *determined*. I believe that God may elect not to know if the person doesn't tell. If you confess to God, if you give thanks to God, then you are open to God. But so many people are not open to God.

Nancey Murphy: I just think it's faulty reasoning to claim that God's foreknowledge determines our actions. We'll just have to leave it there. I don't think I can pursue it any further.

Speaker 4: Part of it seems to me to come from the fact that we take human knowledge and we project that onto God as if God's knowledge were human knowledge to the nth degree. But knowledge in God is not the same thing as it is in us. It's something quite different, which we have no access to. He gives being to all things. But we can't just project knowledge into God, saying that what we know is just projected into God as God's knowledge. That doesn't happen. God doesn't know that way. There is an analogy but the difference is much greater than the similarity.

Speaker 14: The ax I have been grinding for a few years, which nobody seems to pay much attention to, is the interpretation of time and the whole idea of sequentiality and the all-too-human temptation to impose upon God our conception of time. We are stuck with time as a sequential, one-dimensional thing that only runs in one direction. And, therefore, when we talk to one another about things that happen, we are limited in our perception of time to the point that our ordinary way of thinking, way of communication, and everything else is dependent on this unidirectional motion of time. Well, you go out into the land of physics and study general relativity and so forth, you see before you a set of very elegant and beautiful symmetric equations, and all physicists agree, "Boy, it really has to be this way. This is good stuff." Time and space really are equivalent. In the mathematics, in the equations, they are equivalent. And what we have to is be humble enough to recognize that if we, human beings, can write down a bunch of equations and be impressed by them, certainly God can handle that a whole lot better than we can. What we need to do is see it as a limitation of our thought and our communications that time acts the way we perceive it, but God does not necessarily succumb to, or is not restrained by, the human characterization of time. For the entire universe, the space and the time, to be present to God is perfectly reasonable. But it sure doesn't make any sense to humans. So when we get into these situations, as was just brought up here, we have inadvertently limited God to human constraints upon thinking. And that is a big mistake to limit God.

Nancey Murphy: I'd encourage you to grind that ax more often. It's very helpful. The only thing that I would add to it is not to say "our concept of time," but "our concepts." I think we sometimes fool ourselves into thinking that there is *a* concept of time and that somehow the concepts all have to mesh and work together consistently, and they don't. Once every several years you read a book that really changes the way you think. For me one of those was a book by Laycock and Johnson called *Philosophy in the Flesh*. The thesis of the book is that our philosophical concepts are all based on metaphors. For instance, our concept of time depends on the metaphor of time as a road that we are traveling down, or time as a tape that is going past. So that fits with what you are saying. For us it is one-dimensional. But once you recognize that the conceptual network we have for talking about temporality is all structured by means of one or more of these, perhaps consistent, perhaps inconsistent metaphors, then you're much more willing to say, "Oops, we've reached the edge of being able to make sense of this work. We don't know how to extend our metaphors beyond this point and we should stop."

Speaker 4: I just want to go back to Job for a minute. There are two significant things that Job says at the end of the book, which I think are climactic statements. One of these is Job's confession that "I repent of having dealt with things beyond my ability to understand." The second is when he says, "Up to this point in time I have heard about you. Now I know you." There is some profound realization on his part of God's having come into his life at the worst moment of his life and making it meaningful. And that's what the whole Job story seems to be.

Speaker 8: I think you are right on. There is one other thing, though, and that is as you go to the prose section, God commends Job. Recall that he previously challenged Job. As God says twice in the prose section, Job did better than his friends! When Job calls God a cosmic bully, that's better than his friends, who are orthodox and refuse to look at the problem.

Speaker 4: Good, good. The other thing that I think is interesting is that Job always sees everything as coming from God. In this one line that I'm reading, that I really love, he says, "Lord, you're always on my back. You don't give me a chance to spit!" I think that's a beautiful line. It's not the storm, it's not the robbers, it's the Lord. This comes from a course I took in the last year I was in studies at Canton U. It was given by Rod McKenzie, a Jesuit from the Canadian provinces. This was the way he interpreted it.

THERE IS A BREAK IN THE RECORDING HERE AS THE TAPE IS CHANGED. A FEW MOMENTS OF THE DISCUSSION ARE LOST.

Speaker 2: It's easy to understand Christ's miracles, except in one case where there's a change of heart. But when you started talking about your friend I was thinking about the question of miracles, which are difficult to interpret.

Nancey Murphy: There are some words I think we should eliminate from the vocabulary temporarily, until their associations are forgotten and then we can reintroduce them. I think "miracle" is one of those words, because Hume and other friends of the Christian tradition succeeded in getting miracles defined as violations of the laws of nature and set up the problem we've been grappling with ever since. And so I prefer not to use that term, but to speak instead of special divine action meaning something over and above God's ordinary upholding, and providential guiding, of the natural order. As most of you know the original use of miracle in the Bible was that of a sign. It was not a violation of the laws of nature. It was a situation in which God's activity is especially evident. So I think that the Christian tradition means significant events in order to make sense of itself. And so the reason for not simply acquiescing with the liberal Protestant view, such as Scheiermacher's, that either everything's a miracle or everything's a natural event or everything is both is that we really need to make sense of special acts that give us special guidance regarding what God is up to in the world.

Speaker 12: I'm looking at your book and reading about the hard core of self-renunciation. You have provided Simon Weil's list here. I have great trouble following or being in tune with everything that's listed. I can't do it much of the time, I find. I wondered if you could say some things about your experience in dealing with some of these things. You've been looking at these for a number of years. What has been your experience? How do you go about it? What has been the result of it? You have lost a husband and you're in a position, perhaps, to speak about this.

Nancey Murphy: Well, that book, for those of you who don't know, it's the one that George Ellis and I wrote together. It's called *On the Moral Nature of the Universe: Cosmology, Theology and Ethics*. The talk that I gave this morning was a very, very brief synopsis of the sort of argument that we make in that book. It's an argument for a pacifist ethic. I would not have been willing to write such a book by myself. The reason is that it is all too easy for one in my very easy social circumstances, not eligible for the draft, never having been attacked in a dark street, to be dismissed by saying, "You've never been there." And that's true. George Ellis has been deeply involved in the anti-apartheid movement for most of its duration. He knew that he was on a death list. He and his wife kept an apartment outside of the country in case they had to flee in the middle of the night. In fact, I think that George kept a job in Italy part of the time. He seemed always to be working at three places at once, so that he'd have a place to go if he needed to. But I think he and his wife were quite willing to die in the course of what they were doing. They never told us what they did. But when my husband and I spent about ten days in South Africa, so I could finish the book with George, they graciously invited us to live in their home. During the night new people, who had not been there when we went to bed, would be there at breakfast. These were peace activists traveling around. They would tell us of some of the things that George and Mary had done. One of these was to take an old panel truck and paint it white with a red cross and designate it as "Friends' Ambulance Service." They would drive out into the middle of the township violence and pick up black youths who had been shot, because if they ended up in the custody of the authorities they would never survive their injuries. Mary is a physician. It was illegal to treat people with gunshot wounds without turning them over to the authorities. So they [the Ellises] could have been shot or could have been arrested for that. They participated in a variety of activities of that sort. Basically, what I'm doing is trading on George's own experience in living that kind of life. One of the concerns which he raised, and is discussed in the book and for which we have no answer, is: "What provides the strength to keep going?" One question is how to get people involved. That's probably an easier question than the question of: "How do you prevent burnout?" Neither of us feels we have an answer to that on a human level. But the whole concept of a kenotic ethic is one that could never be merely human. So it relies on the faith that God sustains us and that the Holy Spirit works through us when we turn ourselves over to Him in that way.

Chair: I'm going to make only one comment on that book. I just received a copy of that book. The picture on the front is Dresden. As one who has spent four years of my professional life in Germany and part of that in Jena, which is near Dresden, I have some understanding of what happened there. This is a tremendous and moving picture.

Nancey Murphy: That was one of the few instances when the authors got to choose their own photograph.

Chair: I was moved on seeing the cover.

Nancey Murphy: Thanks.

(the book was passed around)

Speaker 2: What is the difference between your position on pacifism and, say, the position of Dorothy Day? Or are you familiar with her and Peter Moran and company?

Nancey Murphy: I don't know that there is any difference. Much of my thinking about pacifism has been shaped by John (Howard) Yoder. I tend to think that if you just read the New Testament, you will become a pacifist without any further complications. But there are variations on the particulars of the why and the whom and the how. I do not know whether John [Howard's] and Dorothy Day's positions differ in detail or not. For a time I would have identified myself as a just war pacifist based on an acceptance of the just war theory, but with the conclusion that no war could ever measure up to the just war standards. So that's a very different pacifism than, say, Yoder's would be.

Speaker 2: I think that is different from Dorothy's.

Nancey Murphy: Yes.

Speaker 2: I had the impression that Paul Feyerabend had sort of returned to metaphysics. He would, of course, never admit that anything was absolute. But I have the impression that you are almost what we would call a positive theologian, in that you do not believe in reason so much as you believe in revelation, and in the data, and you are not going to look for a systematic way of explaining that through the language of a philosophical system. In other words, your approach would be linguistically, rather than systematically, oriented. Is that accurate or is that inaccurate?

Nancey Murphy: That's accurate. I don't have much confidence in philosophical systems. I see philosophy as a second order discipline that basically examines the concepts, reasoning and language of other disciplines, and does not provide us with a body of knowledge.

Speaker 8: As has been said here, your thought is based upon the Bible. My question is whether you suppose that is the way the Bible is? In a sense it is positivistic. There are similarities between that and positivism. Turning it the other way around, the positivists, theologians or philosophers, may have gotten something from the Bible.

Nancey Murphy: The way I got into theology in the first place was by trying to think about theological method: trying to think about the epistemological status of theology. Since I had been studying the philosophy of science before that, my first book was an attempt to show that theological reasoning either is, or could be, isomorphic with scientific reasoning. That is, it is not to be understood rather simplistically as the positivists, or even the neopositivists, would have, but more in the way that Kuhn and Lakatos do. In the course of that I ask, what counts as data for the theologian? and I emphasize particularly the scriptures and religious experience, so long as the religious experience goes through a process of discernment, so that it is not so subjective as individual cognitive experience would be. So I think that an answer to your question is "yes."

III.
Sunday Morning

Speaker 17: I would like you, Nancey, to comment on the present political climate as it relates to the search for scientific and religious truth. I noted here that you connected the anti-evolutionist drive to a moral outrage. It seems to me that there is a lot of power and a meanness going on there. You must have felt some of this with the Johnson and the Board of Trustees incident. I'm not sure if this is something of what Anabaptists and South Africans encountered as they challenged world views and establishments. In the environmental arena, these same moralists have recently thrown down the gauntlet in terms of the Alaska Wildlife Refuge, which many of us consider very holy ground. They have just said "we are going to take it," in order to supposedly have cheap oil. I need some help in seeing how these pieces fit together.

Nancey Murphy: It has surprised me a number of times, when looking into an intellectual issue that seems to have nothing to do with theology, to find that the historical antecedents do, in fact, have to do with competing theologies or competing religious movements. One instance of this is in finding the role of natural theology, if you want to call it theology, played in inspiring Darwin, and has continued to play in sponsoring a particular social agenda. My suspicion is that the fundamentalist movement, which started in America between 1900 and 1920 (I believe), is to some extent responsible for an attitude about intellectual conflict and means of bringing about social change. It seems to have been a particularly combative religious movement, due largely to a sense of being marginalized by progressing society and a sense of being shut out of the halls of power. I shall speak about my students: Most of them are absolutely lovely people, but occasionally in a class of 60 there will be a student who is very rude, vociferous, and outspoken in challenging what I say. I ask, where does this approach to intellectual debate come from? I always think that this is someone too close to the fundamentalist movement to know how we do these things in academia. I don't understand the origins of the fundamentalist movement, but I do think it has conveyed an attitude about intellectual discussion and the necessity of using power in order to get what you want, which continues to today even among people who themselves are not fundamentalists, such as Phillip Johnson.

Speaker 2: I think you are right. And I [will] just relay a very interesting incident at Cosmos and Creation when Langdon Gilkey was our guest. At the conference he talked about the Arkansas school case. This was one of the rulings that were challenged. Someone asked why he thought these people are doing what they are doing. Langdon said he did not know. Then W. Jim Nyhart of the Cosmos group, who comes out of this tradition, said, "I think the reason is fear of atheistic materialism. Because of that sense in the biology books that a sort of attitude can be given to young children that God is out of touch with reality." Langdon responded that this could be right.

Speaker 18: Isn't this true of fundamentalists of all different stripes?

Nancey Murphy: Maybe that is what we mean by fundamentalist.

Speaker 10: Once every other year at Anderson University in my freshman biology class, there will be one student who is hostile and vociferous and so on. We are another one of those gentle and polite campuses with a servanthood tradition. So that always sticks out like a sore thumb. The sense that I get is: 1) there is this self-righteousness about understanding absolute truth against a godless people, and 2) the sense of being a beleaguered minority. This ties in with what you said about Johnson. The creationists view themselves very much as a beleaguered minority, shut out of the main media, the major journals, and ridiculed in the public media. This creates much of a "circle the wagons" mentality. I would like to comment on Johnson's book, *Darwin on Trial*. First, he does not understand biology. Secondly, he plays fast and loose. In critiquing the fossil record, he claims to have heard the rumor of whales being found in Egypt, and then says that he hasn't seen them yet and will just wait to see. All he needs to do is go to the journals. However, there is one thing I still think he did right, which was to expose and document the anti-Christian bias and the contempt in which some of the high priests of secular science hold us. Sometimes it is blatant, and sometimes it is subtle like Steven J. Gould. Not all scientists believe this, but some of their spokespersons do. But the bias exists. So we can understand some of the anger of the young earth people.

Nancey Murphy: That's true. Each side feeds the other. But the mistake that Johnson makes is to say that evolutionary biology is essentially connected with that atheistic rhetoric that shows up in popular writings. Of course it can't show up in a biology journal. So he is making the job harder for people, like me, who want to promote an acceptance of science, and at the same time be critical of people who use science for ideological purposes. There was a move to get him to come and speak on my campus. I said, "over my dead body," because in one night he will undo all of what I have been trying to do in my classes.

Q: What about the freedom of speech implications?

(Laughter)

Nancey Murphy: Well, we don't really have freedom of speech in our classrooms because part of our job is to exercise judgment over what we think our students should be exposed to.

Comment: I am from a state university campus. We had Richard Dawkins as a speaker on our campus. I was shocked by the vociferous, negative, and nasty comments that came out of his mouth, especially when he was challenged in smaller group settings. It was shocking. I just wanted to say that there is this attitude from both sides. There is also a fundamentalism in the scientism people. The scientists, incidentally, were quite upset with Dawkins.

(laughter)

Chair: It is apparent that this discussion could possibly go on forever. I am conscious of the time. There are a number of comments registered. If you feel you really have an important contribution (Laughter) we want to hear from you.

Speaker 19: I was married for 21 years to a fundamental, King James Bible-believing Baptist preacher. I had Ken Hamn, who is the head of the Answers in Genesis movement, in my home for dinner. I fed him a wonderful turkey dinner. I have been indoctrinated in the young-earth creationist ideas. The conflation of evolution with atheism is their main issue. What has always been preached is that if you do not accept a literal version of Genesis Chapter 1 you cannot accept a literal version of Calvary. The two are tied together. Therefore, if you do not take the young-earth creationist view you cannot be saved. Therefore, it is "win at all costs," because we are talking about the salvation of souls. So for me the key to moving beyond that was the uncoupling of that in my relationship to God.

Nancey Murphy: Thanks. That is very helpful.

Speaker 13: This concerns the understanding of the Eucharist. One view is that it is impossible to reconcile divine action and natural processes. But if God created the heavens and the earth, why should God be in competition with the earth? One finds this competition in a lot of Protestant theology. In the fall God curses nature. If you hold the view that nature is devoid of good because of the fall, and waiting to be redeemed. Then thinking about God's presence in nature is a hurdle. If God can be in Jesus and Jesus is in nature, why can't God be in the elements, however you want to understand that? What aspect of this competition of God with the universe do you see in creationism, and what are the roots of that?

Nancey Murphy: I had not thought of the connection with the fallenness of nature. But you may well be right. If nature is fallen, there is a difficulty in thinking of natural processes as embodying God's intentions. You are certainly right to recognize that a strong sense of the sacrimentality of material objects is a good counterbalance to that. But I suspect that the history probably goes back to Enlightenment arguments about divine action in which the emphasis was placed on miracles. I was speaking to the difficulty that modern science creates for understanding that God acts in any way other than writing the laws according to which the universe operates. So if you want to maintain God's special action in human life, you focus on miracles. So we go from saying that there is God's constant action plus miracles, seeing this equated with the laws of nature, which becomes totally uninteresting theologically, to an emphasis on miracles. In the early debates, Hume and so on, the issue was taken to turn on whether there are any miracles, and miracles are defined to be violations of the laws of nature. That means you have given up on the laws of nature themselves as divine action. So I think it is an evolution of views of God's relationship to nature that comes originally from science and gets picked up in early modern philosophy.

Speaker 13: So the creationism is really buying into, albeit unwittingly, this opposition that was set up. So they have, without knowing it, let Hume win the day.

Nancey Murphy: That's right. The irony is that for Newton the metaphor was that the laws of nature were God's commands governing inanimate nature, just as the Ten Commandments are God's laws governing human behavior. The only difference is that nature always obeys and we don't. In a very quick evolution of the understanding of this concept, the laws of nature have a status independent of God. So atheists believe in the laws of nature, even though there is no law-giver. These then become something with which God has to contend if God is to act in the world rather than the means by which God acts.

Speaker 13: Now let me come to the other question. Do you see any relation between views of God's immanence and those theological traditions, which still maintain a sacrimentalist view of nature?

Nancey Murphy: You get interventionism in every Christian group, as far as I know. But I really don't know enough about traditions other than the Catholic. The Catholic Church has maintained a strong sense of sacrimentality and also a strong sense of God's working in all of nature, seeing natural causes as instrumental causes. In fact I can't get some of my Jesuit friends to even see that there is a problem. It's very frustrating.

Speaker 7: Can you help me sort out Chalmers' theodicy and social Darwinism from what your lecture yesterday dealt with about suffering through to a higher good. These are not the same things, I hope anyway. Can you help me sort out why one doesn't lead to the other.

Nancey Murphy: Well, the basic difference is in whether you are accepting suffering as a necessary ingredient in natural or social processes, or if you are imposing suffering on someone else. What Chalmers was about was justifying the imposition of suffering on people.

Speaker 7: It's interesting to learn how theologians and people of faith are learning from evolutionary biologists about the nature of the world. I'm thinking also about how some evolutionary biologists talk about religious faith and the experience of God, and whether it is perceived of as adaptive or not. I am thinking particularly about the Julian James book of about twenty-five years ago: *The Origins of Consciousness and the Breakdown of the Bicameral Mind*. This argues that before the two hemispheres of the brain were able to communicate across the *corpus collosum*, we had this experience of God outside of us. But as the brain matured we outgrew our need for God. There are still these arguments in neuropsychology. I am wondering how we pay attention to these sorts of things. What are your interpretations?

Nancey Murphy: My impression is that there is too quick a jump from neuroscience to religious experience or vice-versa. Philosophers of religion are pretty unclear as to what religious experience amounts to. And there are also differences from one Christian tradition to another, let alone the differences from one religion to another. So I think the first thing to do is sort of a cognitive science analysis of what religious experience is. A useful book that I've used in class was written by Caroline Franks Davis called *The Evidential Force of Religious Experience*. She has a pretty good typology of the kinds of religious experiences within the Christian Religion with some attention to other religions. What's striking about that is the variety of things that can count as a religious experience, such as looking at religious art and having an emotional reaction to it. So it's too much of a "grab-bag" category to talk about "the" neural basis. But there are some general points that we can make. One is to make what I would think is the obvious point, but apparently isn't in the media, that because you can find neurobiological correlates of religious experiences that doesn't mean that we are just making God up. But I actually think you have more to say on that subject than I do. So I welcome any comments you may have.

Comments: You are absolutely right. The biological structuralist equivalent in Newburg, and others, developed the neurological basis out of evolutionary biology continues to acknowledge the validity of religious experience, and even speaks of its adaptive qualities. This is reassuring. There is a school called biogenetic structuralism. Eugene d'Aquilli and Andy Newburg, who is a psychiatrist, are carrying on some of this work.

At his point the book references were asked for.[51]

Speaker 20: This is a question that comes out of the first day. How do we understand the interaction of this supernatural creator with his creation. At one time I thought you had this worked down into something below the quantum indeterminacy level. I thought "God of the gaps." And then you said, no, it was not that. But then I lost where this went. I shall accuse you of a God of the gaps to see where you might go with this, or at least to get the conversation back to that level.

Nancey Murphy: My argument for the action of God at a quantum level is not based on indeterminacy. It is rather the statement that if God acts in everything that exists, then of necessity God acts in the smallest entities or processes. That is simply analytic. So I think that Christian theologians are simply committed to the view that God is immanent in all of God's creation, and is active in some way in all of creation. That is just part of our understanding of the nature of God. But the fact that there is indeterminacy at the quantum level is a bonus for the theologian, because it solves the problem of whether God needs to be seen as intervening. Here let's use intervention in a technical sense meaning, violating the laws of nature. If there are only statistical regularities among these quantum level processes, then a statistical law cannot be violated and you avoid the problem of interventionism. It is not squeezing God in at this rarefied level because the claim is that God is acting at all times in everything. The question is simply, then, how do you reconcile that with science? If the indeterminacy is somehow overturned in quantum physics, the only consequence of that is we are back to the problem of whether or not God must intervene.

Speaker 20: Okay, so the indeterminacy is then strictly tied, in your argument, to the question of whether we must deal with an interventionist view or not.

Nancey Murphy: Right.

Speaker 20: Then let me just ask if you can say anything more about this mysterious thing of God interacting with the physical realm. Of course, as Christians and scientists this seems very interesting.

Nancey Murphy: As Austin Farrer, philosopher of religion, is famous for pointing out that we can never understand the causal joint, as he calls it, between God and the world. That is, we have no way of understanding how God makes something happen because God's action is unique. However, if one postulates that God acts by affecting the outcome of quantum processes, then you can raise some fairly meaningful questions about what sorts of events one ought to see in the macroscopic world as a result of divine action. You may or may not be aware of the series of conferences the Vatican Observatory has sponsored over the years. The last one was on quantum physics. So most of the discussion at that conference was on questions of the possible macroscopic effects of divine action at the quantum level. John Polkinghorne is famous for having said that you simply do not get anywhere with divine action at the quantum level because the effects all wash out at the macroscopic level. So the question is what constitutes a measurement and what are the macroscopic consequences of that? My knowledge of quantum physics does not permit me to repeat the conclusions of that group. I urge you to look for the book when it comes out. It will be published by CTNS (The Center for Theology and the Natural Sciences). But there was general agreement that this is not an implausible view of how God acts at the macroscopic level. I would love to hear from some physicists who can speak knowledgeably about the macroscopic/quantum level interface. Do we have a volunteer?

Speaker 21: Well, I was going to ask a question that is somewhat related. Yesterday, you seemed to be making a rather important point that God's action at the macroscopic level with human beings was a respecter of their persons accepting the costs. You seem to have made the same point at the microscopic level. That is, God respects the particle. This reminds me of the statement at the turn of the century that the microcosm repeats the macrocosm. Atoms were like these little solar systems. But that was a big dead end. What occurs at the microscopic level is nothing like what occurs at the macroscopic level. That why you have such a hard time understanding it. A lot of people understand Einstein's theory of relativity. But even Richard Feynman once said that nobody understands quantum theory. So where do we get this principle that God's action with humans would be the same as God's action with particles? Is this a principle from philosophy that we want to have there? It is not justified from the scientific side is what I am saying.

Nancey Murphy: No, it's not intended to be justified scientifically, but rather expecting that there is some consistency in how God treats all of God's creatures. But of course adjusted to take into account the type of creature it is. And so I talk of there being an analogy between indeterminacy at the quantum level and freedom at the human level. The subtitle I've given to the paper where I've written about this was "Buridan's and Balaam's Asses." The point of the title was I was arguing that it does make sense for God to affect Buridan's ass's choice of which pile of hay to eat, rather than standing and starving because each one was equally attractive. Not all of you are familiar with the mythology of the philosophical tradition. Buridan was a medieval philosopher. Although he did not actually invent this example, it is attributed to him. So it is called Buridan's ass. It was a thought experiment in order to pursue the question of the principle of sufficient reason. You have a donkey that is hungry and you stand him equally distant between two equal piles of hay. Will he choose one, or will he stand there and starve to death for lack of sufficient reason to choose one or the other? And so I use that as an analogy to say that God can determine the outcome of otherwise indeterminate quantum events. However, I would reject the story of Balaam's ass being required to speak because although donkeys do regularly choose piles of hay, they do not regularly speak. So I was going to say that I wouldn't take the Balaam's ass story as having any historical significance. But that is the point I was going to make. Nick Saunders, in a critique of my views published in *Zygon*, claims that, at the quantum level, one simply cannot make sense of the requirement of these basic constituents having natures of their own. That is, their natures are determined by what they do. I am just not at a point in my knowledge of physics to know if that is a valid criticism or not. So this is an idea at least thought to have originated with W.G. Pollard, and has been kicked around by a number of theologians for a number of years. The first I heard of it was reading Ian Barbour's critique of Pollard and dismissing the idea. And so I am interested to see that, as a result of some of the pieces a number of us have written recently, it is an idea that is being considered again. But it is one that has to be considered by a team of thinkers which includes physicists. This cannot be pursued any further by someone like me.

Chair: I acknowledge the looks you gave me as you mentioned quantum theory. I do, of course, teach quantum theory and have some ideas here. But I prefer at this time to provide discussion time for others.

Speaker 22: I really appreciate the way you have faced, with honesty, a lot of difficult questions. I see that as refreshing. You have also been honest when you are not sure what the status of certain things is. Having studied some theology I also appreciate the use of scientific reasoning and methods of testing in theology. A parallel question regards the nature of death as discussed by Frans de Waal. Can you say something to that?

Nancey Murphy: His central point is to contest the idea of nature as "bad natured." He speculates that certain Calvinistic understandings of the fall lie behind the interpretation of nature as vicious. He is basically an ethologist and is reporting a lot of his observations of animal behavior.

Speaker 22: I am trying to draw a parallel from a philosopher's perspective. This is similar to what I heard Don Knuth talk about in a conference for mathematicians. If one considered a set of interacting artificial intelligences and asked how it would be best to interact with these artificial intelligence's, Knuth suggested that it would be easiest to be one of them. This is not to imagine that one is God, but to try to see things from God's perspective.

Nancey Murphy: Thanks.

Speaker 10: I have a full issue and a quip. There was a comment about Richard Dawkins and about how nasty and aggressive he was. I talked with Richard Lewontin once, a Harvard geneticist who is not particularly sympathetic to Christianity. He said that Dawkins isn't even a scientist. He is simply one who makes his money saying outrageous things. So, it seems that, in the scientific community, Dawkins isn't held in very high esteem. As I think more about this question of God's immanence as opposed to intervention. It follows that if God is immanent he is probably working at the most useful level, and the reason we still see a lot of suffering and the messiness is that God works in a non-coercive way. The thing I am struggling with a bit is, if we say God is non-coercive as one way to address the problem of theodicy, it almost seems to me that we are back to where we have been before. That is, saying that God gets the laws of nature going; he very seldom violates them because he respects his creation; he is not going to be coercive and that is why we get natural evil, such as earthquakes, famine, disease, and so on. That is, out of humility, God steps back and doesn't coerce his creation doing what we would consider good. That, to me, seems to be going back to justifying natural evil by saying that God is non-coercive. It's almost like pulling him back out, saying he is not really immanent, he's there and he chooses not to intervene. So I'm chasing this idea in circles.

Nancey Murphy: It is really trying to split the difference between two positions, neither of which seems to be theologically acceptable. You can say that God only works by upholding the natural processes, and they are law-governed, and that gets you off the hook for natural evil. For some reason, God has simply chosen to only act in this way. Then you lose any sense that God actually has to do with us personally on a day-to-day basis. You don't have any account of how God can answer prayer, except perhaps inspiring you to pray for things that were going to happen anyway. If you are physicalist, God can't inspire you without tampering with your brain somehow. So there just isn't any way to maintain the Christian sense of God's action in history if you stick strictly with divine action through the processes of nature. But if you take the interventionist view that God can and does simply violate the laws of nature whenever God chooses, then the problem of evil becomes unmanageable because you can't answer the question, "why doesn't God intervene regularly to prevent natural disasters?" What I have tried to do is produce an account of how God acts that reproduces our Christian sense that most of the time most of what happens is regular and orderly in the natural world, and yet there are indeed events that we can attribute in some special way to divine action. But I do this without taking an interventionist route. It's like all positions that are trying to walk a tight rope between two problematic alternatives. It may or it may not be stable. It might be that you can't stay on that tightrope. Theologically, I think we are compelled to try.

Speaker 9: Haught says that God plays dice with the universe because God wants the universe to be other than God. If God and the universe were one, that would be pantheism. So God does what he does because God wants the universe to be other than God. In pantheism God is still above; he still preserves his transcendence. But God is not identical with the universe. That is the way Haught says it. Does that sound possible?

Nancey Murphy: It sounds true and valuable, but it still doesn't provide any answer to the question of how God is doing it when he is active in the universe. How is that reconciled with our sense of the orderliness of nature?

Speaker 9: Getting back to the fundamentalists. They are called fundamentalists because they have five doctrines that they fundamentally believe. I know your position on dogma and doctrines. But it seems to me that there has to be some core belief in any religious tradition. That's a core belief that maybe doesn't change. For us Catholics it's almost the same as for you Mennonites, except for the Eucharistic aspect. I would like to know what you think, in the light of our evolutionary theology today, about the development of doctrine. That is, just from your standpoint?

Nancey Murphy: One of my long-standing interests, since I studied both philosophy and theology, is the extent to which doctrine has been shaped by philosophical developments, for good or for ill. I've written a book where I've attempted to understand theological method, and you could say theological development or doctrinal development, on the model of the development of scientific research programs. What you are saying about an essential core of things that don't change fits perfectly into my account of theological method. Lakatos talks about research programs having what he calls "the hard core," which is a sort of metaphysical commitment regarding the nature of the reality you are studying. He claims that to give that up is essentially to give up the program. But that leaves you free to make alterations in what he calls the auxiliary hypotheses in response to data that don't fit the program. I would still hold to that as a pretty good description of how theologies change over time, but with the addition that reform movements, or other kinds of radical changes, come along within a religious tradition that essentially start new programs. I think you can say the Lutheran tradition starts with a revolution and changes what counts as the central core of Christian teaching.

Speaker 9: So the original sin that we have been talking about here, used to be a very core doctrine and we are still wrestling with it in our own church. The article I wrote is all about a misnomer about original sin. In the Easter vigil services in the Catholic Church next Saturday they are going to say, "Oh, necessary sin of Adam that brought such a great redeemer." That makes Adam's sin an afterthought for God. God came down because of an afterthought. I subscribe to John Duns Scotus' idea that God was always meant to come to the universe. And by the way the Pope just deified Duns Scotus in 1993. A little late! He must have liked Duns Scotus' idea that God always meant to come to the universe and it wasn't the original sin of this hominid that made Christ come. That's really going to change the doctrine of original sin. That can not be a core belief anymore because of the evolutionary theology. That's my point. I wonder what you think about that?

Nancey Murphy: I agree. I think that's great. We talk about the doctrine of sin, but it's a strange thing to have a doctrine about.

Speaker 9: About a mythical couple that did this. So taking the history of Adam and Eve as literally true.

Nancey Murphy: Many theologians have distinguished between the fall as an historical event and fallenness, or the term "the fall," taken as standing for the sinful character of human nature without identifying it with the first sin.

Speaker 4: Just a brief comment. That was to the discussion about quantum and freedom. There is a marvelous chapter in Karl Schmitz-Moorman's book, which I mentioned earlier, on the evolution of freedom, in which this is considered in a very beautiful way. It is a great book on Evolution of Freedom, Evolution of Information, Evolution of Consciousness.

Chair: Karl was a Catholic theologian.

Speaker 4: Yes.

Speaker 23: There is this fascinating business we bumped into when Gerald Schroeder's book was mentioned, and then also when mention was made in essence regarding God's perspective versus our perspective, in which we are stuck on this one way time line. Flatland occurs to me. The chain of causality, which we find so dear in science, obviously from God's perspective isn't even there. Frankly, this little series of comments is directed to what has just transpired. If we are going to, in one setting, recognize that things that are in scripture and talk about God's being are timeless or out of time, we must realize that, when we bump into them, they are going to be hard to express in human terminology. We are stuck in this scenario in which parts of scripture appear to be historical, at least in the sense of telling a series of sequences. From God's perspective, that was not [necessarily] sequential [just] because that is what we're stuck with. I found that my ears went up when Nancey and a couple of others were talking about the events surrounding the fall. Whether it's literal or historical or not, it seems that the message that's there [regards] the nature of the relationship between man, that special creation of God, and the Creator. This underwent some kind of significant change, some kind of degradation, and then the physical realm and creation have suffered ever since. I just felt then that we played a little fast and loose with causal change. Under some circumstances causal change is okay, and under some other circumstances we are ready to abandon causal change.

Speaker 14: I recall that in your lecture, shortly after you put that "tree thing" on the board with all the "bad guys" in the branches, somehow or other you locked together the creationists and the antiabortionists. I was terribly puzzled as to how that connection was made.

Nancey Murphy: No, I think you misheard. I moved from there to talk about Phillip Johnson's particular interests having to do with sexual morality, sexual roles and homosexuality, but I don't think I mentioned abortion. But I would guess that's equally a part of the "Johnson and other intelligent design" agenda. It goes along with traditional family values.

Speaker 14: My own view of course is an anti-abortion one, but it comes from a point of view that within the realm of evolution, and all the things that are up there on the board [claiming] that God acts through nature and so forth. Once conceived, provided you don't attack and kill it, you get an ordinary person like the rest of us. There is no shift away from natural biology involved in trying to say that the unborn have a right to life. I am aware that there are folks in the traditional family-values thing who coincide with pro-life or anti-abortion positions. But I certainly thought there was a connection there that lumped a bunch of people together that really didn't really have that close a connection. You are saying that I misheard you at that point.

Nancey Murphy: Umhmm [yes].

Speaker 23: You didn't give much attention to Number 5 – the two worlds. I think some things can be said in defense of that, at least to say that we should be cautious about hitching theology a little bit too much to the prevailing view in science. We have seen in the past there is some mischief that attends those projects. For example, that of Thomas Aquinas, who was so impressed by Aristotle that he created a synthesis which compromised, I think, some basic biblical beliefs. And the same thing has happened in connection with Sir Isaac Newton in the Newtonian era when people felt so great about this harmony of science and faith in depth of deistifying, if I can use that word, Christianity. So too now we should sit a little more loosely with respect to what is going on in evolution, because that is changing also. We might have to revise our theology if we tie it too closely to certain currently prevailing views about evolution.

Nancey Murphy: I think one needs to distinguish between the details of scientific positions and the general view of reality that one gets if you stand back and let the details blur a little bit. But we are constantly in danger of getting something wrong theologically, whether we pay attention to science or not. It just seems to me that the more we try to know of a non-theological nature, as we do in our theology, the more likely we are to come out with a good theology. The attempt to avoid relating theology to science for a long time, I think, resulted in worse theological blunders in some cases than say [those of] Thomas did. I think that Bultmann is a case in point. So your caution is well taken, but I am busy leaning in the other direction.

Speaker 18: In this respect can you really decouple culture from theology, because you are living in the world? As a consequence, whenever there is a huge paradigm shift, for example from the Newtonian to the quantum, you are really affected. Also the views [we have culturally] are embedded, whether we want [them to be] or not, in theology. Therefore, should we not allow theology also to become an evolutionary kind of activity?

Nancey Murphy: Yes, I think that's a good point. We've only got the concepts we've got to think with. And science is going to affect those concepts no matter what. The more explicit we are in recognizing their scientific origin the more intelligent we can be about what we say theologically. It's parallel to the arguments between some Protestant theologians and others, saying that theology should not be done with the aid of philosophy. Well, you might be able to exclude inclusion of certain philosophical systems, but you are going to be affected by the philosophy of your age whether you know it or not. It's better to know it.

Speaker 18: Could we not use Lakatos' idea of core beliefs as those that are really essential and almost immutable, and those at the periphery that are now susceptible to evolution and change?

Nancey Murphy: I think that's useful so long as you don't make the mistake that Carnak did of thinking you can make a sharp distinction between the kernel and the husk.

Notes

[1] Goshen College is located in Goshen, Indiana. It is one of five undergraduate institutions of higher education of the Mennonite Church, USA.

[2] See, for instance, Joel B. Green, "Bodies – That is, Human Lives: A Re-Examination of Human Nature in the Bible," in Warren S. Brown, Nancey Murphy, and H. Newton Malony, eds., *Whatever Happened to the Soul? Scientific and Theological Portraits of Human Nature* (Minneapolis: Fortress Press, 1998), 149-174.

[3] J.D.G. Dunn, *The Theology of the Apostle Paul* (Grand Rapids: Eerdmans, 1998), 51ff.

[4] Most often cited is Oscar Cullmann, *Immortality of the Soul or Resurrection of the Dead? The Witness of the New Testament* (London: Epworth Press, 1958).

[5] For a helpful overview, see Francisco J. Ayala, "Human Nature: One Evolutionist's View," in Brown et al., eds., *Whatever Happened to the Soul?*, 31-48.

[6] Thomas Aquinas, *Summa Theologica*, Ia, 75-83.

[7] Joseph LeDoux, *The Emotional Brain: The Mysterious Underpinnings of Emotional Life* (New York: Simon and Schuster, 1996).

[8] Quoted by Alwyn Scott, *Stairway to the Mind: The Controversial New Science of Consciousness* (New York: Springer Verlag, 1995), 81.

[9] See Leslie Brothers, *Friday's Footprint: How Society Shapes the Human Mind* (New York: Oxford, 1997).

[10] Paul Churchland, *The Engine of Reason, The Seat of the Soul: A Philosophical Journey into the Brain* (Cambridge, MA: MIT Press, 1995), 132-143.

[11] Peter Hagoort, "The Uniquely Human Capacity for Language Communication: From POPE to [po:p] in Half a Second," in Robert J. Russell, Nancey Murphy, Theo C. Meyering, and Michael A. Arbib, eds., *Neuroscience and the Person: Scientific Perspectives on Divine Action* (Vatican City State and Berkeley: Vatican Observatory and Center for Theology and the Natural Sciences, 1999), 45-56.

[12] Antonio R. Damasio, *Descartes' Error: Emotion, Reason, and the Human Brain* (New York: G.P. Putnam's Sons, 1994), 8.

[13] *Ibid.*, 10.

[14] Fraser Watts, "Cognitive Neuroscience and Religious Consciousness," in Russell, et al., eds., *Neuroscience and the Person*, 327-346.

[15] John Hunston Williams, *The Radical Reformation* (Philadelphia: Westminster Press, 1962), chap. 23.

[16] *Ibid.*, 581.

[17] Wolfhart Pannenberg, *Jesus – God and Man* (Philadelphia: Westminster Press, 1968).

[18] James Wm. McClendon, Jr., *Ethics: Systematic Theology, Volume 1* (Nashville, TN: Abingdon Press, 1984), 89.

[19] James Wm. McClendon, Jr., *Doctrine: Systematic Theology, Volume 2* (Nashville, TN: Abingdon Press, 1994), 151.

[20] *Ibid.*, 149.

[21] Nicholas Lash, *Easter in Ordinary: Reflections on Human Experience and the Knowledge of God* (Charlottesville, VA: University Press of Virginia, 1986).

[22] David Kelsey, *The Uses of Scripture in Recent Theology* (Philadelphia: Fortress Press, 1975), 159.

[23] McClendon, *Doctrine*, 268.

[24] John Howard Yoder, *He Came Preaching Peace* (Scottdale, PA: Herald Press, 1985), 91.

[25] New York: Harper and Row, 1968.

[26] I argue this point in my *Beyond Liberalism and Fundamentalism: How Modern and Postmodern Philosophy Shape the Theological Agenda* (Valley Forge, PA: Trinity Press International, 1996).

[27] For an excellent overview of the problem, see Russell's introduction in Robert J. Russell, Nancey Murphy, and C.J. Isham, eds., *Quantum Cosmology and the Laws of Nature: Scientific Perspectives on Divine Action* (Vatican City State and Berkeley: Vatican Observatory and Center for Theology and the Natural Sciences, 1993).

[28] See, for example, Gordon Kaufman, "On the Meaning of 'Act of God,'" *Harvard Theological Review* 61 (1968): 175-201.

[29] In *Before the Beginning: Cosmology Explained* (London and New York: Boyars/Bowerdean, 1993), 89-90. For a full account, see John D. Barrow and Frank J. Tippler, *The Anthropic Cosmological Principle* (Oxford: Oxford University Press, 1988).

[30] This is Philip Hefner's term. See *The Human Factor* (Minneapolis: Fortress, 1993).

[31] This is Howard Van Till's term; see "When Faith and Reason Meet," in Michael Bauman, ed., *Man and Creation: Perspectives on Science and Theology* (Hillsdale, MI: Hillsdale College Press, 1993), 141-164.

[32] I am not the first to suggest that God acts in the natural world by influencing the

otherwise undetermined behavior of subatomic entities. See, for example, W.G. Pollard, *Chance and Providence* (New York: Scribner, 1958).

[33] I deal with some of these issues at greater length in "Divine Action in the Natural Order: Buridan's Ass and Schroedinger's Cat," in Russell, et al., *Chaos and Complexity,* 407-436.

[34] See *Science and Providence: God's Interaction with the World* (Boston: Shambhala, 1989), 66-67.

[35] Holmes Rolston, III, "Does Nature Need to Be Redeemed?" *Zygon,* 29, no. 2 (June, 1994): 205-29; quotations 218-20.

[36] In *Power and Responsibility* (Chicago: Henry Regnery Co., 1961), 62.

[37] *The Traces of God in a Frequently Hostile World* (USA: Cowley Publications, 1981), 35.

[38] Here we come back to the issue addressed in "God's Nonviolent Direct Action."

[39] See Ian Barbour, *Issues in Science and Religion* (New York: Harper and Row, 1966).

[40] Phillip E. Johnson, *Darwin on Trial* (Washington D.C.: Regnery Gateway, 1991).

[41] This is the interventionist versus immanentist distinction that I made in "God's Nonviolent Direct Action."

[42] Robert T. Pennock, *Tower of Babel: The Evidence Against the New Creationism* (Cambridge, MA: MIT Press, 1999).

[43] Phillip E. Johnson, *Reason in the Balance: The Case against Naturalism in Science, Law, and Education* (Downers Grove, IL: InterVarsity Press, 1995).

[44] Darwin, quoted in Robert M. Young, *Darwin's Metaphor: Nature's Place in Victorian Culture* (Cambridge: Cambridge University Press, 1985), 41.

[45] Darwin's notes, quoted in Young, op. cit., 41f.

[46] Thomas Chalmers, *The Adaptation of External Nature to the Moral and Intellectual Constitution of Man,* 2 vols. Bridgewater Treatises (London: Pickering, 1833), 292f.

[47] Young, *Darwin's Metaphor,* 191.

[48] Frans de wall, *Good Natured: The Origins of Right and Wrong in Humans and Other Animals* (Cambridge, MA: Harvard University Press, 1996), 80.

[49] See my account in "God's Nonviolent Direct Action."

[50] Hans Hut, quoted in Rollin S. Armour, *Anabaptist Baptism: A Representative Study* (Scottdale, PA: Herald Press, 1966), 78.

[51] The references were: **Caroline Franks Davis,** *The Evidential Force of Religious Experience;* **Eugene d'Aquilli,** *The Spectrum of Ritual: A Biogenetic Structural Analysis;* **Eugene d'Aquilli and Andy Newburg,** *The Mystical Mind: Probing the Biology of Religious Experience*

Index

A

Adam and Eve, 80
Alaska Wildlife Refuge, 95
Allen, Diogenes, 41
amygdala, 17
Anabaptist thinking, 44
Anabaptists, 95
Answers in Genesis movement, 98
anti-apartheid movement, 91
Aquinas, 13, 16, 59, 111
Ardipithecus ramidus, 15
Aristotle, 13, 111
atheism, 31
Augustine, 13, 41
Australopithecus afarensis, 15
Australopithecus anamensis, 15

B

Barbour, Ian, 45, 62, 105
Behe, Michael, 46
Biblical anthropology, 13
biblical perspective, 82
biblical point of view, 82
binding problem, 17
blessing, 68
Bohr, 70
Bracken, Joseph, 60

O

occasionalism, 32
Old Earth Creationists, 44
original sin, 108

P

Paley, William, 48
pan-experientialism, 61
Pannenberg, Wolfhart, 21, 63, 65
pan-psychism, 61
peace and nonviolence, 28
Pennock, Robert, 47
physicalism, 11, 20
physicalist, 106
Pick, John, 85
Platonic soul, 13
Polkinghorne, John, 36, 60, 103
Pollard, William, 78, 105
Pope, 108
positivistic, 94
power, 79
prayer, 85, 106
prey, 82
process philosophy, 71
process theology, 60
Progressive Creationism, 44
Provider, 31
Psychopannychia, 21

Q

quantum level, 59, 102
quantum physics, 103
quantum theory, 76

The Speaker

Nancey Murphy is Professor of Christian Philosophy at Fuller Theological Seminary, Pasadena, California. She received a B.A. from Creighton University (philosophy and psychology) in 1973, a Ph.D. from U.C. Berkeley (philosophy of science) in 1980, and a Th.D. from the Graduate Theological Union (theology) in 1987.

Her first book, *Theology in the Age of Scientific Reasoning* (Cornell, 1990) won the American Academy of Religion award for excellence and a Templeton Prize for outstanding books in science and theology. She is author of five other books, including *Reconciling Theology and Science: A Radical Reformation Perspective* (Pandora Press, 1997), *Anglo-American Postmodernity: Philosophical Perspectives on Science, Religion, and Ethics* (Westview, 1997); and *On the Moral Nature of the Universe: Theology, Cosmology, and Ethics* (with G. F. R. Ellis, Fortress, 1996). She has co-edited six volumes, including *Whatever Happened to the Soul?: Scientific and Theological Portraits of Human Nature* (with Warren Brown and H. N. Malony, Fortress 1998); and *Neuroscience and the Person: Scientific Perspectives on Divine Action* (with Robert Russell, Theo Meyering, and Michael Arbib).

Her research interests focus on the role of modern and postmodern philosophy in shaping Christian theology, and on relations between theology and science. She is on the Board of Directors of the Center for Theology and the Natural Sciences and former chair of the board. Murphy is an ordained minister in the Church of the Brethren.